BELGIUM

THROUGH

THE AGES

A CONCISE GUIDE

By

Martin Miller-Yianni

COPYRIGHT AND ACKNOWLEDGEMENTS

Publisher: Martin Miller-Yianni, Yambol, Bulgaria

First Printing Edition 2024

ISBN 978-619-7742-51-0 (paperback)
ISBN 978-619-7742-52-7 (ePub)

A CIP catalogue record for this book is available from:

The National Register of Published Books in Bulgaria
bulevard 'Vasil Levski' 88,
1504 Sofia,
Bulgaria

Cover Image:
Waterside, Antwerp, Belgium by Libby-Penner from unsplash.com

Title Page Image:
St. Joseph - The Patron Saint of Belgium (www.eglise st joseph.be)

PREFACE

'Belgium Through the Ages: A Concise Guide' offers an authentic reflection of Belgium's unique stories of the past. As the first part of a series on the history of various nations, this book stands out for its dedication to accuracy and detail, while remaining accessible to a wide range of readers. The author has visited Belgium many times and feels a deep connection to its history.

One of the book's key strengths is its thoughtful structure. Each chapter covers important historical eras yet acknowledging the overlapping nature of many events. There are also recaps of significant events within chapters to ensure clarity and cohesion. These selective repetitions help readers see how events from different time periods interconnect and influence one another.

The author guides readers through Belgium's historical transitions, summarising pivotal moments to maintain the narrative flow. This approach helps contextualise the intricate forces that have shaped the nation over the centuries. Whether readers are looking for a deeper understanding of specific eras or a broad overview of Belgium's historical evolution, this book provides a wealth of reliable knowledge giving insightful analysis.

From the achievements and challenges of ancient societies to the cultural transformations of modern times, each chapter immerses readers in Belgium's historical development, offering a well-rounded view of the nation's journey to the present day.

The author's personal connection to Belgium enriches the narrative, adding a layer of authenticity and passion to the historical account. Additionally, the book is designed with numerous sections that can be easily referred to for quick information, making it a practical resource for both casual readers and serious history enthusiasts.

CONTENTS

The state coat of arms of Belgium, adopted on 17 March 1837, is a symbol of national identity and unity. Its origins trace back to the Duchy of Brabant, where the Leo Belgicus or Belgian Lion, a golden lion rampant on a black field, was a prominent symbol.

Historical Background

After gaining independence from the Netherlands in 1830, Belgium sought national symbols reflecting its heritage. The lion of Brabant was chosen for its association with courage and sovereignty, a common emblem in the heraldry of the Low Countries.

Description and Symbolism

The coat of arms features the Leo Belgicus in gold on a black shield, with red claws and tongue. This colour scheme is mirrored in the national flag of Belgium. Supporting the shield are two lions guardant, each holding a lance with the national flag, symbolising strength and vigilance. Above the shield is a royal crown, representing Belgium's constitutional monarchy. The grand collar of the Order of Leopold surrounds the composition and beneath the shield is a red ribbon with the national motto, "L'union fait la force" (Unity makes strength), in French, Dutch and German.

Variations and Usage

There are greater, middle and lesser versions of the coat of arms. The greater arms, used by the monarch, include additional elements like a mantle with ermine lining and banners of the nine provinces. The middle and lesser arms are simplified versions for government use. The coat of arms appears on official documents, government buildings and currency, symbolising Belgium's unity and strength.

THE FLAG OF BELGIUM

The national flag of Belgium, adopted on 23 January 1831, is a tricolour consisting of three vertical bands of black, yellow and red. These colours are derived from the coat of arms of the Duchy of Brabant, symbolising the nation's heritage and struggle for independence.

Historical Background

The flag's origins are linked to the Belgian Revolution of 1830, when the country sought independence from the Netherlands. Initially, the flag featured horizontal stripes, but it was later changed to vertical stripes, influenced by the French Tricolour, a symbol of liberty and unity.

Description and Symbolism

The flag's design features three equal vertical bands: black nearest the hoist, followed by yellow and red. The unusual proportions of 13:15 make it distinctive. The black represents the shield, the yellow the lion and the red the lion's claws and tongue from the Brabant coat of arms.

Variations

The flag is used in various forms, including the civil ensign and state ensign, which feature additional symbols like a lion rampant. The naval ensign has a different design, incorporating a yellow saltire on a white field with black and red borders.

Usage

The flag is prominently displayed on government buildings, official documents and during national celebrations, symbolising Belgium's unity and pride.

Belgium, officially known as the Kingdom of Belgium, is a small yet significant country in Northwestern Europe. It is bordered by the Netherlands to the north, Germany to the east, Luxembourg to the southeast and France to the south. To the west, it has a short coastline along the North Sea.

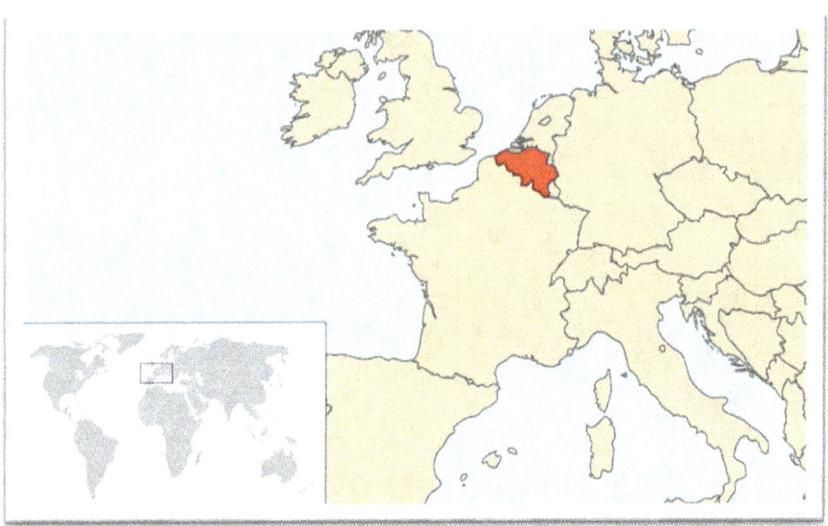

Geographical Position

Belgium's geographical coordinates are approximately 50°50'N latitude and 4°00'E longitude. The country covers an area of 30,689 square kilometres (11,849 square miles), making it one of the smaller European nations. Despite its size, Belgium's strategic location has made it a crucial hub for international politics, commerce and culture.

Regions and Topography

Belgium is divided into three main regions: Flanders in the north, Wallonia in the south and the Brussels-Capital Region in the centre. The country's topography includes the coastal plain in the northwest, the central plateau and the Ardennes uplands in the southeast. The coastal area features sandy beaches and dunes, while the central plateau is characterised by fertile valleys and rolling hills. The Ardennes region is known for its rugged terrain and dense forests.

Climate and Environment

Belgium experiences a temperate maritime climate, with mild winters and cool summers. The North Sea influences the weather, bringing moderate rainfall throughout the year. The country's rivers, including the Meuse and the Scheldt, play a vital role in its geography and economy.

BELGIUM: THE LAND AND PEOPLE

Belgium, a small yet historically significant nation in northwestern Europe, has often found itself at the crossroads of major European political, cultural and economic developments. Known for its diverse landscapes, rich cultural heritage and complex social fabric, Belgium offers a fascinating case study of how geography, history and human endeavour can intertwine to shape the character of a nation. In this chapter, we will explore Belgium's geography and the nature of its people, shedding light on how both have shaped and been shaped by historical events.

GEOGRAPHY OF BELGIUM

Belgium, covering a modest 30,528 square kilometres, is often described as a "small country with big contrasts." Despite its limited size, Belgium's landscape is remarkably diverse. The country can be divided into three main geographical regions: the coastal plains in the northwest, the central plateau and the Ardennes highlands in the southeast.

The coastal region, characterised by flat, sandy plains, is lined by the North Sea. This area, particularly Flanders, has historically been a hub for commerce and industry, with cities such as Bruges and Ghent flourishing as medieval trading centres. Over time, this region has evolved into an urban and industrial heartland, benefiting from its proximity to the sea and neighbouring nations like the Netherlands.

Moving inland, the central plateau of Belgium offers a fertile and gently undulating landscape. This region, known for its agriculture, is the backbone of the country's farming industry. In addition to being agriculturally productive, the central plateau is also home to Belgium's most populous cities, including the capital, Brussels. This area has been instrumental in shaping the modern identity of Belgium, both politically and economically.

Finally, the Ardennes in the southeast presents a striking contrast with its dense forests, rolling hills and rocky outcrops. This area is less populated and more rugged, historically providing a natural barrier to invasions from the south. The Ardennes is a region of scenic beauty, offering a different pace of life compared to the bustling cities of the north. Although less industrialised, it has become popular for tourism and outdoor activities.

Belgium's geographic location at the heart of Europe has always made it a strategic area for trade, migration and conflict. Its borders, shared with France, Germany, Luxembourg and the Netherlands, place it at the junction of several major European powers. This positioning has been both a blessing and a curse, as Belgium has often been the site of European conflict, but it has also allowed the country to become an important hub for diplomacy and trade in modern times.

THE PEOPLE OF BELGIUM

Belgium's population is an intricate mosaic of languages, cultures and communities, reflecting the country's complex historical evolution. With a current population of over 11 million, Belgium is home to two primary linguistic groups: the Dutch-speaking Flemish community, which resides mainly in the northern region of Flanders and the French-speaking Walloon community, predominantly located in the southern region of Wallonia. A smaller German-speaking minority exists in the east, close to the German border.

This linguistic divide is central to understanding Belgium's identity. The Flemish and Walloons, while living in the same country, maintain distinct cultures, languages and traditions, often leading to tensions regarding political and economic representation. These differences have manifested in various forms of regionalism and even calls for greater autonomy or independence in certain quarters. The capital city of Brussels, officially bilingual but predominantly French-speaking, serves as a microcosm of the country's complexity, acting as a symbol of Belgium's unity while also reflecting its inherent divisions.

THE BELGIAN PEOPLE

The Belgian people are known for their cultural diversity and resilience. Belgium's history has been marked by periods of foreign domination, from the Spanish and Austrian Habsburgs to French and Dutch rule. Each of these powers left an imprint on Belgium's cultural and social development, contributing to the rich makeup of Belgian identity. In the modern era, Belgium became an independent state in 1830 and since then, its people have navigated the challenges of nation-building, balancing regional identities with the demands of a centralised state.

The industrial revolution in the 19th century had a profound impact on the social structure of Belgium. The growth of coal mining, steel production and textiles, particularly in Wallonia, transformed the country into one of Europe's early industrial powerhouses. This period saw significant urbanisation, with many Belgians moving from rural areas to cities in search of work. The working class, especially in Wallonia, became increasingly politicised, giving rise to strong socialist movements and demands for social reform.

Belgium's urban centres today, such as Brussels, Antwerp and Liège, reflect this industrial heritage. However, they are also hubs of contemporary European culture, with vibrant arts scenes, world-class cuisine and bustling international communities. Brussels, in particular, stands out not only as the capital of Belgium but as the de facto capital of the European Union, hosting a range of EU institutions and international organisations. This status reinforces Belgium's global outlook and its people's engagement with wider European and international affairs.

Despite the regional differences, certain aspects of Belgian culture are shared across the country. Belgians are known for their love of fine food and drink, with the country being world-renowned for its chocolate, beer and waffles. Additionally, Belgium has produced a range of internationally recognised artists, musicians and writers, from the surrealist painter René Magritte to the comic book hero Tintin, created by Hergé. Sports, especially football and cycling, are also an integral part of Belgian life, bringing communities together in a shared national pride.

Prehistoric Beginnings and Ancient Times

c. 400,000 BCE - 500 CE

Belgium, though a relatively small nation today, has a rich history that stretches back thousands of years, long before it emerged as a distinct political entity. The prehistoric and ancient periods of Belgium's history are marked by significant human activity,

CAVE PAINTINGS FOUND IN BELGIUM

cultural shifts and external influences, which together laid the foundation for its later development. In this section, we will explore the early human settlement of the region, the role of Celtic tribes, particularly the Belgae and the transformative impact of Roman conquest and occupation.

Early Human Settlement

Belgium's earliest human history can be traced to the Paleolithic era, as evidenced by archaeological discoveries of ancient tools, weapons and cave art. Human activity in the region dates back to around 400,000 years ago, when Neanderthals roamed the forests and plains of what is now Belgium. The most significant finds from this era come from the famous caves of Spy, located near the Meuse River, where well-preserved Neanderthal remains and tools were discovered in the late 19th century. These findings provide crucial insights into the daily lives, survival strategies and migratory patterns of early humans during the Ice Age.

NEANDERTHAL REMAINS FROM THE CAVES OF SPY

As the climate warmed and the Ice Age retreated, the Mesolithic period brought new waves of human settlement. Small, nomadic groups of hunter-gatherers established themselves in Belgium's forests, rivers and coastal areas. These groups adapted to the changing environment, hunting game such as deer and boar while also exploiting the region's rich waterways for fishing.

By the Neolithic period (c. 5000 BCE), there was a marked shift from a hunter-gatherer lifestyle to one of farming and permanent settlement. The introduction of agriculture—likely spread from other parts of Europe—allowed communities to grow, leading to the construction of small villages. One notable archaeological site from this period is at Spiennes, in the province of Hainaut. Here, a large Neolithic flint mine, one of the oldest in Europe, has been unearthed. Spiennes is now recognised as a UNESCO World Heritage site, testifying to the sophistication of early Belgian settlers in their use of tools and resource management.

Celtic Tribes and Belgic Influence

By the Iron Age (c. 800 BCE), the region that is now Belgium was populated by various Celtic tribes, most notably the Belgae, a confederation of tribes that would leave a lasting mark on the area. The Belgae were part of the broader Celtic culture that spanned much of Western and Central Europe, known for their distinctive art, warrior traditions and social organisation. They inhabited what would become northern France, Belgium and southern Britain.

The Belgae, from whom Belgium derives its name, were a warlike people who fiercely defended their territory from external threats. Julius Caesar famously described them in his 'Commentarii de Bello Gallico' (Commentaries on the Gallic War) as "the bravest of the Gauls," a testament to their reputation as formidable warriors. The Belgae established strong tribal communities and their society was characterised by a hierarchical structure with a noble warrior class, druids (who acted as priests and arbiters) and commoners engaged in farming and trade.

Culturally, the Belgic tribes left a significant imprint on the region, developing a distinct identity that separated them from other Celtic groups. They constructed hillforts and fortified settlements, often strategically located along rivers and trade routes. Evidence of Belgic craftsmanship, such as their finely wrought metalwork, pottery and coinage, has been found at numerous archaeological sites across Belgium. Their extensive trade networks connected them with other Celtic regions and Mediterranean civilisations, suggesting that early Belgian tribes were not isolated but were part of broader European interactions.

Roman Conquest and Legacy

The Roman conquest of Gaul, led by Julius Caesar between 58 and 50 BCE, marked a turning point in the history of Belgium and the wider region. Following his campaigns, Belgium—then known as Gallia Belgica—was incorporated into the Roman Empire. The Belgic tribes, despite their resistance, were eventually subdued by the superior organisation and military might of the Romans. This conquest would have a profound and lasting impact on the region, transforming its social, economic and political landscape.

Under Roman rule, Gallia Belgica became a highly Romanised province, benefiting from the introduction of Roman law, governance and infrastructure. The Roman legacy in Belgium can be seen in the extensive road networks they built, which facilitated trade and military movement across the region. These roads, many of which followed ancient Celtic paths, connected towns like Tongeren (Atuatuca Tungrorum), the oldest city in Belgium, with major Roman centres such as Cologne and Trier. The town of Tournai, too, became an important hub of Roman administration.

Trade flourished under Roman occupation, as Belgium became integrated into the vast Roman economic system. The region was rich in resources such as iron, timber and agricultural products, which were exported across the Empire. In return, Belgium benefited from the influx of goods from the Mediterranean, including wine, olive oil and pottery. Roman villas and towns sprung up across the countryside, reflecting the growing wealth of the region's Romanised elites.

The Romans also introduced a new architectural and urban planning style to Belgium, the remnants of which can still be seen today. Archaeological sites such as the Roman baths at Chaudfontaine and the remains of a Roman villa at Mettet are examples of the sophisticated lifestyle enjoyed by some of Belgium's inhabitants during this period. Tongeren, with its grand forum and amphitheatre, remains a key site for understanding Roman urbanism in the region.

Religion and culture were also transformed during Roman rule. The Roman pantheon of gods, temples and festivals became intertwined with local Belgic traditions, leading to a syncretism of beliefs. Roman citizenship and Latin culture spread among the elite and Latin eventually became the administrative language of the region, although Belgic dialects persisted in rural areas.

Despite the relative stability and prosperity brought by Roman rule, the region was not immune to external threats. By the late 3rd century CE, the Roman Empire was in decline and Germanic tribes such as the Franks began to push into Roman territory. The fall of the Roman Empire in the West by the 5th century left a power vacuum in Belgium, which would soon be filled by these new groups, setting the stage for the medieval period. Keeping the same information, double the word count

THE REMAINS OF A ROMAN VILLA AT METTET

The Roman Empire brought a period of relative stability and prosperity to the region, but it was not entirely free from external threats. By the late 3rd century CE, the Roman Empire was experiencing a decline, and Germanic tribes such as the Franks began to encroach upon Roman territory. This period of instability continued, and by the 5th century, the Western Roman Empire had fallen, leaving a significant power vacuum in the region now known as Belgium.

This vacuum was soon filled by various Germanic tribes, including the Franks, who began to establish their own rule and influence over the area. This transition marked the beginning of the medieval period in Belgium, characterised by the gradual integration of Roman and Germanic cultures and the formation of new political entities. The decline of Roman authority and the subsequent rise of Germanic powers set the stage for the complex and dynamic history of medieval Belgium.

SUMMARY:

Belgium's history begins with its early human settlers during the Paleolithic period, with evidence of hunting and tool-making activities. By the Iron Age, the region was inhabited by Celtic tribes, notably the Belgae, after whom the Romans named the area. The Roman conquest in 57 BCE by Julius Caesar marked the start of Romanisation, with Belgium becoming part of Gallia Belgica. Roman rule brought the construction of roads, cities like Tongeren (the oldest in Belgium) and an introduction to Latin culture. However, the collapse of the Western Roman Empire in the 5th century left the region vulnerable to invasions by Germanic tribes like the Franks.

DID YOU KNOW?

The discovery of the Scladina Cave in Wallonia revealed Neanderthal remains dating back over 100,000 years, showing that prehistoric Belgium was inhabited far earlier than many previously believed. The Scladina Cave excavation has offered rich insights into the life and tools of early humans in Belgium, with discoveries of stone tools and evidence of long-term Neanderthal presence.

PEOPLE:

Julius Caesar (100–44 BCE) - Roman general who conquered the Belgae and incorporated the region into the Roman Empire.

Ambiorix (1st century BCE) - Leader of the Eburones tribe, known for leading a revolt against Roman forces.

Celtic Tribes - The Belgae, Nervii, Eburones and Menapii tribes inhabited the region before Roman conquest.

PLACES:

Tongeren - Oldest city in Belgium, founded by the Romans.

Gallia Belgica - Roman province covering modern Belgium, Luxembourg and parts of northern France.

Ardennes - Region of dense forests inhabited by Celtic tribes, later a key battleground during Roman campaigns.

EVENTS:

Roman Conquest of Gaul (57 BCE) - Julius Caesar's campaign to subdue the Belgae.

Ambiorix's Revolt (54 BCE) - Uprising by the Eburones tribe, temporarily defeating Roman legions.

Collapse of Roman Empire (5th century CE) - Led to the region's integration into the Frankish kingdoms.

CHAPTER 2

THE MIDDLE AGES AND THE RISE OF THE LOW COUNTRIES

500 CE – 1500 CE

The Middle Ages were a transformative period for the region now known as Belgium, shaping its political, social and economic structures in profound ways. Following the collapse of the Roman

MIDDLE AGE PEASANT LIFE

Empire, Belgium entered a period of significant change, during which new political entities formed, Christianity spread and powerful duchies like Flanders and Brabant began to emerge. Feudalism became the dominant social and political system, leading to the creation of a hierarchical society and the foundation of Belgium's medieval identity. This section explores the post-Roman transition, the rise of Christianity, the development of powerful duchies and the social order under feudalism in medieval Belgium.

Post-Roman Transition and Early Christianity

The fall of the Western Roman Empire in the 5th century marked the beginning of a new era for Belgium. The region, which had been part of the Roman province of Gallia Belgica, saw the collapse of Roman administrative structures and the gradual retreat of Roman influence. In the vacuum left by the Romans, new Germanic tribes, particularly the Franks, began to settle in the area. The Franks, a confederation of tribes from the Lower Rhine region, would become the dominant power in northern Gaul, establishing what would eventually become the Frankish Kingdom.

Under the leadership of King Clovis I, the Merovingian dynasty of the Franks unified much of Gaul, including what is now Belgium, in the late 5th and early 6th centuries. Clovis' conversion to Christianity, likely influenced by his wife Clotilde, a Christian princess, marked a turning point in the religious history of the region. Following Clovis' baptism, Christianity spread rapidly among the Frankish elite, leading to the establishment of the Church as a powerful institution in the emerging Frankish state. This conversion also aligned the Franks with the Roman Catholic Church, distinguishing them from other Germanic tribes that remained pagan or adhered to Arianism.

In the centuries that followed, the Christianisation of Belgium progressed steadily. Missionaries, most notably Saint Servatius and Saint Lambert, played a key role in converting the local population and establishing Christian communities. By the 8th century, the region was firmly within the sphere of the Catholic Church. Monasteries and abbeys, such as Stavelot and Lobbes, became centres of religious, intellectual and economic life, preserving knowledge through scriptoria (manuscript-copying centres) and providing vital services such as education and care for the poor.

The Carolingian dynasty, which succeeded the Merovingians in the 8th century, further strengthened Christian institutions. Charlemagne, the most famous Carolingian ruler, expanded his empire to cover much of Western Europe, including Belgium. His reign saw a revival of learning and the arts, known as the Carolingian Renaissance, with Belgium benefiting from the increased stability and cultural exchange.

CHARLEMAGNE'S CAROLINGIAN EMPIRE ENCOMPASSED MOST OF WESTERN EUROPE

THE GROWTH OF FLANDERS AND BRABANT

As the Carolingian Empire fragmented following Charlemagne's death, Belgium experienced the rise of powerful local rulers. By the 9th and 10th centuries, the duchies of Flanders and Brabant had emerged as dominant political entities in the region. Both Flanders, in the west and Brabant, in the centre and east, would play a crucial role in the economic and political development of medieval Belgium.

Flanders, in particular, became one of the most prosperous and densely populated areas in Europe during the High Middle Ages. The fertile land and access to the North Sea made Flanders an important agricultural and commercial hub. Bruges, Ghent and Ypres grew into significant urban centres, supported by a booming textile industry that relied on wool imports from England. These cities became key nodes in the emerging network of European trade routes, attracting merchants from across Europe and beyond. The growing wealth of these cities gave rise to powerful urban elites, who often challenged the authority of the nobility and sought greater autonomy for their towns.

Brabant, though less commercially focused than Flanders, also developed into a powerful duchy. Its position as a crossroads between the Low Countries, the Holy Roman Empire and France made it a key player in regional politics. Brussels, the capital of Brabant, began to grow as a centre of governance and trade. Brabant was known for its relative stability and strong ducal authority, which contrasted with the more fragmented political landscape of Flanders, where rival factions frequently vied for power.

The urbanisation of Belgium during this period was a key factor in its economic and political development. Towns and cities grew around markets, trade routes and ecclesiastical centres, leading to the rise of a wealthy merchant class. The development of guilds, which regulated trades and crafts, also contributed to the economic prosperity of the region. These guilds held significant political influence in the towns, often forming alliances with the urban elite to resist the control of local lords and assert their rights and privileges.

THE FEUDAL SYSTEM AND SOCIAL ORDER

The political and social landscape of medieval Belgium, like much of Europe, was shaped by the feudal system. Feudalism, which emerged following the collapse of the Carolingian Empire, was a system based on land ownership and personal loyalty. In this hierarchical structure, the king granted large estates (fiefs) to nobles in exchange for military service. These nobles, in turn, granted portions of their land to vassals, who were typically knights or lower-ranking lords. At the bottom of the social hierarchy were the peasants, who worked the land and provided food for the upper classes.

In Belgium, the feudal system was marked by significant regional variation. Flanders, with its wealthy and independent cities, often saw tensions between urban centres and feudal lords. The counts of Flanders, who ruled over much of the region, were powerful figures, but they often faced challenges from the cities, which sought to assert their economic and political independence. This tension was particularly evident during the late 12th and early 13th centuries, when the cities of Flanders, led by Bruges and Ghent, formed leagues to resist the authority of the counts. These urban revolts were a precursor to the more organised resistance of the later medieval period, which saw cities like Ghent play a key role in regional power struggles.

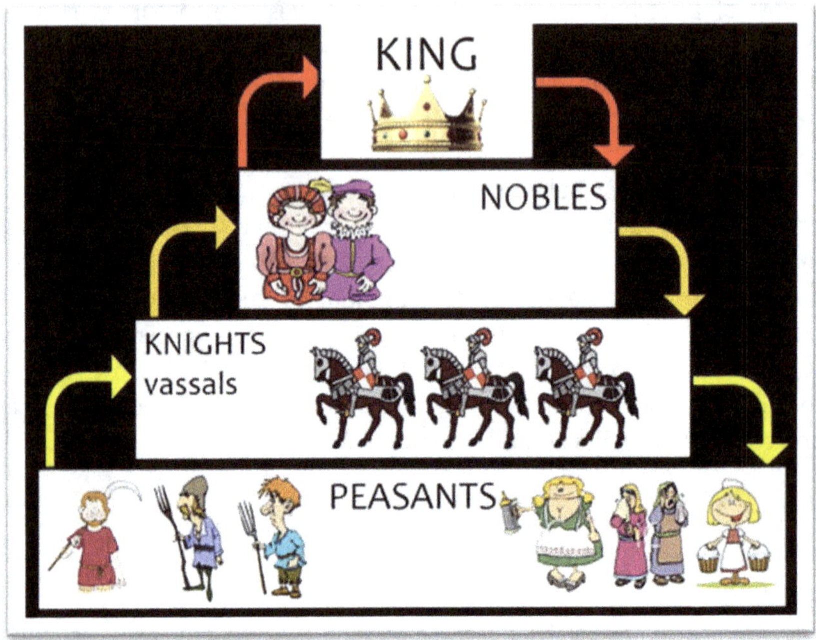

THE FEUDAL SYSTEM

In contrast, the duchy of Brabant was characterised by a more cooperative relationship between the nobility and the cities. The dukes of Brabant recognised the economic importance of their urban centres and often granted charters and privileges to cities like Brussels and Leuven, which allowed them a significant degree of autonomy. This relative harmony between the nobility and the urban population contributed to the political stability and prosperity of Brabant during the Middle Ages.

Social order in medieval Belgium was also shaped by the Church, which held considerable influence over the lives of both peasants and nobility.

Monasteries were not only religious centres but also played a key role in agricultural production, education and healthcare. The Church reinforced the feudal hierarchy through its teachings, which emphasised the divine right of kings and the duty of subjects to obey their lords. However, the Church also provided a degree of social mobility, as individuals from humble backgrounds could rise to positions of power and influence within the Church hierarchy.

By the 13th century, feudalism in Belgium was undergoing significant changes. The emergence of powerful cities and the expansion of trade and commerce began to undermine the traditional feudal order. Wealth and influence were increasingly concentrated in urban centers rather than being tied solely to land ownership. This shift marked a departure from the old feudal system, where land was the primary source of power and wealth.

In rural areas, feudal relations continued to exist, with lords and vassals maintaining their traditional roles and obligations. However, the cities of Flanders and Brabant were at the forefront of a new era. These urban centres developed more sophisticated systems of governance, reflecting the growing importance of commerce and trade. Councils composed of merchants, guilds, and nobles began to share power, creating a more balanced and complex political structure.

The rise of these cities brought about significant social and economic changes. Merchants and guilds gained influence and began to play a crucial role in the governance of the cities. This shift in power dynamics led to the development of new political institutions and practices. The collaboration between different social groups in the urban councils marked a departure from the hierarchical and land-based power structures of the feudal system.

SUMMARY:

After the fall of Rome, Belgium was integrated into the Merovingian Frankish Kingdom and later into the Carolingian Empire under Charlemagne. By the 9th century, feudalism took hold and the region was divided into small duchies and counties, including Flanders, Brabant and Hainaut. From the 12th to the 14th centuries, Belgian cities like Bruges,

Ghent and Ypres became prosperous trading hubs, especially known for wool and textiles. The Battle of the Golden Spurs (1302), where Flemish forces defeated the French army, symbolised the growing power of the Low Countries' urban elites.

DID YOU KNOW?

The city of Bruges was once one of the wealthiest cities in Europe and one of the world's main commercial hubs during the 12th and 13th centuries. Bruges was the focal point of the Hanseatic League's trade network, particularly in the wool and cloth industry, fostering a cosmopolitan environment that made it a centre of economic and cultural exchange.

KEY PEOPLE, PLACES AND EVENTS OF THE ERA

PEOPLE:

Charlemagne (742–814) - Born in the region of modern Belgium, his Carolingian Empire encompassed most of Western Europe.

Baldwin I of Flanders (c. 830–879) - Founder of the County of Flanders, a key political entity in the region.

Jacques van Artevelde (1290–1345) - Flemish statesman and leader of Ghent during its conflict with France.

PLACES:

Bruges - Major medieval trading city and a key member of the Hanseatic League.

Ghent - A centre of textile production and political power in medieval Belgium.

Ypres - Another prominent medieval city, famous for its cloth trade.

Abbey of Stavelot - Important religious centre in medieval Belgium.

EVENTS:

Battle of the Golden Spurs (1302) - Flemish forces defeated the French near Kortrijk, marking a rise in Flemish independence.

Rise of the Hanseatic League (12th–14th centuries) - Flemish cities became key players in this commercial alliance.

Hundred Years' War (1337–1453) - Impacted trade and politics in the Low Countries, with Flemish cities caught between France and England.

THE BURGUNDY ERA

1384 - 1482

*T*he Burgundian Era (1384-1477) marked a pivotal period in the history of the Low Countries, including modern-day Belgium. During this time, the region experienced significant political unification under the powerful Burgundian dukes, leading to a flourishing of culture, art and economic activity. This era also laid the foundation for future

THE HOUSE OF BURGUNDY

political developments in the Low Countries. However, the sudden death of Charles the Bold and subsequent inheritance disputes eventually brought an end to Burgundian rule, leading to the Low Countries coming under Habsburg control. We will now explore the rise of the Burgundian state, its cultural and economic impact and the political upheaval that followed the end of Burgundian dominance.

THE RISE OF THE BURGUNDIAN STATE

The rise of the Burgundian state in the Low Countries was a result of a series of strategic marriages, alliances and inheritances that began in the late 14th century. The first major turning point occurred in 1384, when Philip the Bold, Duke of Burgundy, married Margaret III, Countess of Flanders. This marriage brought several key territories in the Low Countries—Flanders, Artois and the County of Burgundy—under Burgundian control. Over the next century, the Burgundian dukes expanded their influence through a combination of diplomacy, inheritance and conquest, eventually unifying much of what is today Belgium, the Netherlands and Luxembourg.

The Burgundian dukes were vassals of the French crown, but they were often more powerful than many of the French king's other subjects, controlling a vast and wealthy domain. Philip the Bold's successors—John the Fearless, Philip the Good and Charles the Bold—consolidated and expanded their control over the Low Countries, acquiring territories such as Brabant, Hainaut, Holland and Zeeland through marriage alliances and the careful management of regional politics. By the mid-15th century, the Burgundian state had become a formidable power, with its capital in Brussels and a highly centralised administration.

The political implications of this unification were profound. The Burgundian dukes introduced a more centralised form of government in the Low Countries, replacing the patchwork of feudal lordships and city-states with a unified administration. They established institutions such as the States General, a representative assembly that included delegates from the various provinces under Burgundian rule. Although the States General was initially a tool of the dukes, it laid the groundwork for the development of a more cohesive political identity in the Low Countries. The Burgundians also created a professionalised bureaucracy to oversee their expanding territories, improving the efficiency of tax collection, trade regulation and military organisation.

However, the centralisation of power also led to tensions with the independent-minded cities of Flanders, Brabant and Holland. These cities had long enjoyed a high degree of autonomy and the Burgundian efforts to curb their independence often resulted in conflicts. The most notable of these was the Bruges Revolt of 1436-1438, during which the citizens of Bruges rebelled against the heavy taxes imposed by Philip the Good. While the revolt was ultimately crushed, it demonstrated the limits of Burgundian authority and foreshadowed future unrest in the region.

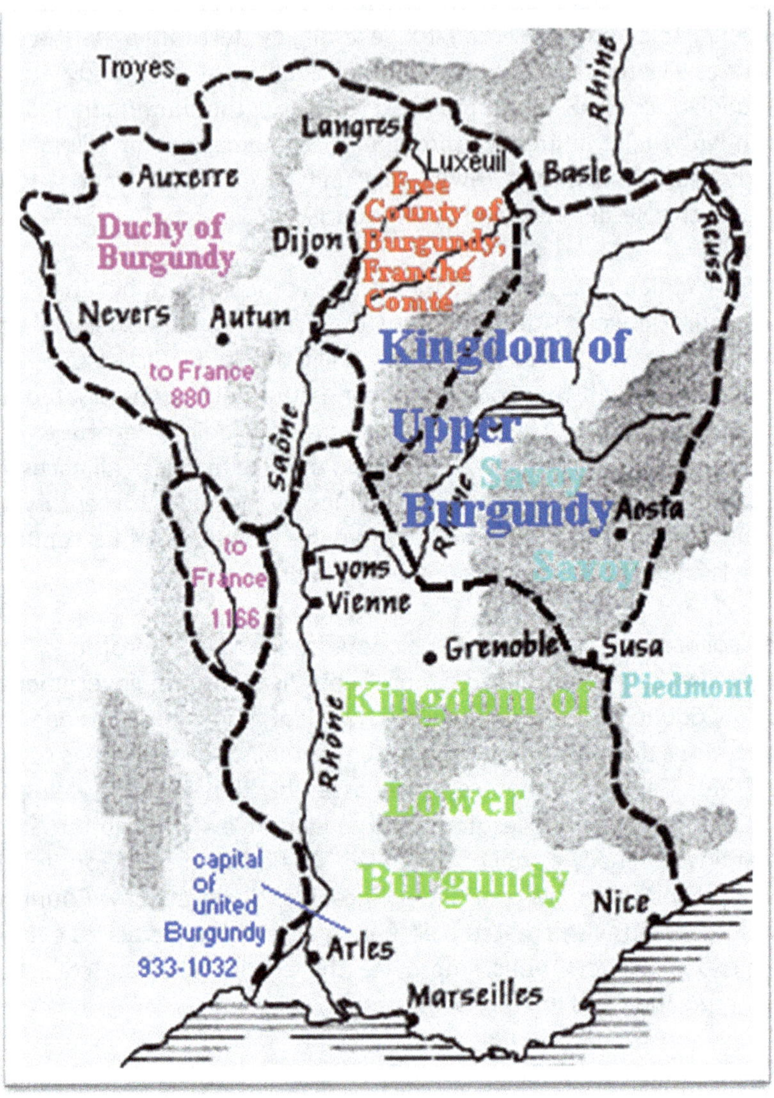

MAP OF THE BURGUNDY KINGDOM

Cultural and Economic Flourishing

Despite the political tensions, the Burgundian period was one of unprecedented cultural and economic growth in the Low Countries. The cities of Flanders and Brabant, particularly Bruges, Ghent and Antwerp, became centres of commerce, finance and artistic production. Bruges, in particular, flourished as a major international trading hub, attracting merchants from across Europe and beyond. Its strategic position along the North Sea and its access to the English wool trade made it a focal point for the burgeoning textile industry, which brought immense wealth to the city.

Antwerp, too, rose to prominence during the Burgundian era, benefiting from its position on the River Scheldt and its growing importance as a centre for trade and finance. By the late 15th century, Antwerp had eclipsed Bruges as the economic heart of the Low Countries, becoming one of Europe's most important commercial cities. The influx of wealth into these cities fuelled the growth of a prosperous merchant class, who became influential patrons of the arts and culture.

The Burgundian court itself was a major patron of the arts, attracting some of the most talented artists, musicians and writers of the time. Philip the Good, in particular, was a notable patron and his court in Brussels became a vibrant cultural centre. The Burgundian dukes were known for their lavish lifestyle and their courts were filled with magnificent tapestries, illuminated manuscripts and ornate jewellery. The Burgundian court also fostered the development of the Northern Renaissance, which was characterised by a focus on realism, detailed portraiture and religious themes.

One of the most significant artistic legacies of the Burgundian period was the development of the Flemish school of painting. Artists such as Jan van Eyck, Rogier van der Weyden and Hans Memling revolutionised the art of painting with their use of oil paints, intricate details and mastery of light and texture. Their works, often commissioned by wealthy patrons in Bruges and Ghent, reflected both religious devotion and the burgeoning material wealth of the region. Van Eyck's 'Arnolfini Portrait' and

Memling's 'Last Judgement' are prime examples of the artistic achievements of this period.

The Burgundian dukes also played a significant role in shaping the musical culture of the Low Countries. The Burgundian court employed some of the finest musicians and composers of the age and it was during this period that the Franco-Flemish school of polyphony emerged. Composers such as Guillaume Dufay and Gilles Binchois became famous for their contributions to sacred and secular music, influencing the development of Renaissance music across Europe.

THE END OF BURGUNDIAN RULE

The Burgundian state reached the height of its power under Charles the Bold, the last of the Burgundian dukes. Charles was an ambitious ruler who sought to expand his territories and elevate his domain to the status of a kingdom. His aggressive expansionist policies, however, led to conflicts with his neighbours, particularly France and the Swiss Confederacy. Charles' military campaigns against these powers ultimately proved disastrous and his ambitions exceeded his military capabilities.

In 1477, Charles the Bold was killed at the Battle of Nancy while fighting against the Swiss and their allies. His death marked the sudden end of Burgundian ambitions in the Low Countries. Charles died without a male heir, leaving his vast territories to his daughter, Mary of Burgundy. This succession led to a series of inheritance disputes, as various European powers, most notably France, sought to claim parts of the Burgundian inheritance.

Mary of Burgundy's marriage to Maximilian of Habsburg, the future Holy Roman Emperor, in 1477 ensured that the Low Countries would remain under Habsburg control, rather than falling to the French crown. This marriage effectively transferred the Burgundian territories to the Habsburg dynasty, setting the stage for the future political landscape of Europe. The Habsburgs, through Mary's son Philip the Fair, would eventually inherit not only the Low Countries but also Spain and its overseas empire, creating one of the most powerful dynasties in European history.

SCENE PAINTED OF THE BATTLE OF NANCY

However, the transition from Burgundian to Habsburg rule was not without challenges. The cities of the Low Countries, particularly in

Flanders, were wary of the new Habsburg rulers and resisted attempts to centralise authority further. Mary of Burgundy herself faced rebellions from cities like Ghent and Bruges, which sought to preserve their traditional privileges and autonomy. While the Habsburgs eventually secured control over the region, the tensions between central authority and local autonomy would continue to shape the history of the Low Countries in the centuries to come.

SUMMARY:

The 15th century saw the unification of the Low Countries under the powerful Dukes of Burgundy, beginning with Philip the Good. This era, known as the Burgundian Netherlands, marked a golden age for art, trade and culture. Cities like Bruges and Antwerp flourished as European commercial centres, while artists like Jan van Eyck and Rogier van der Weyden produced masterpieces in the burgeoning Flemish Renaissance. The court of the Dukes of Burgundy was one of the most opulent in Europe and their patronage encouraged the growth of the arts. However, the death of Charles the Bold in 1477 led to the region being inherited by the Habsburgs through marriage.

*** * ***

DID YOU KNOW?

Philip the Good, Duke of Burgundy, founded the Order of the Golden Fleece in Bruges in 1430. This chivalric order became one of the most prestigious in Europe, symbolising the wealth, power, and culture of Burgundy, which had turned the Low Countries into a highly influential political and cultural region.

KEY PEOPLE, PLACES AND EVENTS OF THE ERA

PEOPLE:

Philip the Good (1396–1467) - Duke of Burgundy who unified the Low Countries and promoted the arts and commerce.

Charles the Bold (1433–1477) - Last Duke of Burgundy, whose death ended Burgundy's control of the region.

Jan van Eyck (c. 1390–1441) - Flemish painter, considered a master of Early Netherlandish painting.

Rogier van der Weyden (1400–1464) - Flemish painter who gained prominence during the Burgundian rule.

PLACES:

Bruges - Cultural and commercial hub under Burgundian rule.

Antwerp - Emerged as a significant trading city, especially after the decline of Bruges' port.

Dijon - Capital of the Duchy of Burgundy, though Bruges was its economic heart.

EVENTS:

Treaty of Arras (1435) - Secured Burgundian independence from France and allowed Philip the Good to consolidate power.

Union of the Burgundian Netherlands (1433) - Philip the Good unites various counties and duchies, including Flanders, Brabant and Luxembourg.

Death of Charles the Bold (1477) - His death at the Battle of Nancy ended the Burgundian dynasty and led to Habsburg control of the region.

CHAPTER 4

HABSBURG RULE AND THE SPANISH NETHERLANDS

1482 - 1713

*T*he 16th and 17th centuries were a time of significant political, religious and social upheaval in the Low Countries, including what is today Belgium. Under Habsburg rule, the region

THE HABSBURG DYNASTY

experienced growing religious tensions between Catholics and Protestants, culminating in the Eighty Years' War, which eventually split the northern and southern Netherlands. Belgium, as part of the Spanish Netherlands, remained under Catholic Habsburg control, where the Counter-Reformation played a key role in shaping society. The Habsburg ascendancy will be examined, the impact of the Eighty Years' War and the influence of Spanish governance and Catholicism on Belgium during this period.

The transition to Habsburg rule in the Low Countries began in 1477 with the marriage of Mary of Burgundy to Maximilian of Habsburg. Their union brought the Burgundian territories, including the Low Countries, under Habsburg control. By the early 16th century, the Habsburgs, under Emperor Charles V, held a vast empire that included not only the Holy Roman Empire but also Spain and its overseas colonies. The Low Countries became part of this sprawling empire and Charles V, born in Ghent, considered the region one of his most prized possessions.

Charles V's reign (1519-1556) saw the consolidation of Habsburg power in the Low Countries. He introduced reforms aimed at centralising governance, reducing the autonomy of the provinces and strengthening royal authority. However, his policies often conflicted with the strong tradition of local self-governance in the cities of Flanders, Brabant and other provinces. Additionally, the region's economic prosperity, particularly in cities like Antwerp, gave rise to a powerful merchant class that resented increased taxation and external control.

Religious tensions began to escalate during Charles V's reign, as the Protestant Reformation spread across Europe. By the mid-16th century, Protestantism, especially Calvinism, had gained a significant foothold in the Low Countries, particularly in the urban centres of Flanders and Brabant. The region's proximity to Protestant strongholds in Germany and the influx of Protestant ideas via trade routes contributed to this religious shift. Calvinism appealed to many merchants, artisans and urban elites, who saw in it both a spiritual alternative to Catholicism and a vehicle for social and political change.

Charles V, a devout Catholic, saw Protestantism as a threat to the unity of his empire and responded with harsh measures to suppress it. His successor, Philip II of Spain, who inherited the Low Countries in 1555, continued this policy with even greater zeal. Philip's efforts to enforce Catholic orthodoxy, combined with his attempts to centralise power and raise taxes, exacerbated tensions in the Low Countries. His appointment of the Duke of Alva as governor in 1567, with orders to crush Protestantism, only inflamed the situation further. Alva's use of the

"Council of Blood" to persecute Protestants and dissenters, as well as the imposition of heavy taxes, provoked widespread resistance.

CHARLES V TRIED TO REFORM BUT WITH CONFLICT

THE EIGHTY YEARS' WAR

The growing religious and political tensions reached a breaking point in 1568 with the outbreak of the Eighty Years' War, a protracted conflict between the Protestant northern provinces and the Catholic Spanish Habsburgs. The war, also known as the Dutch Revolt, was both a struggle for religious freedom and political independence. While the northern provinces of the Low Countries, led by the Dutch Republic, sought to break away from Spanish rule, the southern provinces—what is now Belgium—remained more divided in their loyalties.

During the early years of the conflict, much of the fighting took place in the southern Low Countries, where cities like Antwerp and Ghent became key battlegrounds. However, over time, the southern provinces, which were predominantly Catholic, came to favour reconciliation with Spain. The Union of Arras in 1579 formalised this alignment, as several southern provinces agreed to remain loyal to the Spanish crown and support the Catholic cause. In contrast, the northern provinces formed the Union of Utrecht, declaring their independence from Spain and establishing what would eventually become the Dutch Republic.

The war had a profound impact on the southern Netherlands. The city of Antwerp, once a major economic centre, suffered severely during the conflict. In 1585, the Spanish forces, led by the Duke of Parma, recaptured Antwerp after a prolonged siege. The city's fall marked a turning point in the war, as many Protestant merchants and intellectuals fled north to the Dutch Republic, further weakening the economy of the southern provinces. Antwerp's decline as a commercial hub allowed Amsterdam, in the north, to rise as the new centre of trade and finance.

By 1609, the war had settled into a stalemate, with the northern Netherlands effectively independent and the southern provinces under firm Spanish control. The Twelve Years' Truce, signed in 1609, temporarily halted the fighting, but the final peace came only with the Treaty of Westphalia in 1648. This treaty officially recognised the independence of the Dutch Republic and confirmed the division of the Low Countries into two separate entities: the Protestant Dutch Republic in the north and the Catholic Spanish Netherlands in the south.

THE COUNTER-REFORMATION AND SPANISH INFLUENCE

In the aftermath of the Eighty Years' War, the Spanish Netherlands, which included modern-day Belgium, became a stronghold of Catholicism. The Spanish Habsburgs, deeply committed to the Counter-Reformation, implemented policies aimed at reinforcing Catholic orthodoxy and suppressing any remaining Protestant influence. The Catholic Church played a central role in shaping the cultural, religious and social life of the region during this period.

One of the most significant aspects of Spanish rule was the vigorous promotion of the Counter-Reformation, a movement within the Catholic Church aimed at countering the spread of Protestantism and revitalising Catholicism. The Jesuits, a Catholic religious order founded during the Counter-Reformation, were particularly influential in the Spanish Netherlands. They established schools, seminaries and missions throughout the region, focusing on education and the re-evangelisation of the population. The Jesuits also played a major role in the arts, sponsoring religious works that emphasised the themes of piety, obedience and the glory of the Catholic Church.

The impact of the Counter-Reformation was especially visible in the architecture and art of the period. Baroque churches, characterised by their grandeur and elaborate decoration, were constructed in many cities, reflecting the Catholic Church's desire to inspire awe and reinforce its authority. In Brussels, Antwerp and other major cities, religious art flourished under the patronage of both the Church and the Spanish crown. Artists such as Peter Paul Rubens and Anthony van Dyck became leading figures in the Baroque movement, creating dramatic and emotional religious works that celebrated the triumph of Catholicism.

Rubens, in particular, played a central role in the cultural life of the Spanish Netherlands. As a court painter to the Archdukes Albert and Isabella, the Spanish governors of the region, Rubens produced masterpieces that reflected both religious themes and the political power of the Habsburg rulers. His works, such as 'The Descent from the Cross' and 'The Elevation of the Cross', exemplify the Baroque style, with its emphasis on movement, emotion and grandeur.

The Catholic Church also influenced social life in the Spanish Netherlands. Religious festivals, processions and ceremonies became important public events, reinforcing the sense of Catholic identity. The Church's emphasis on charity and social welfare led to the establishment of hospitals, orphanages and other charitable institutions, which provided care for the poor and vulnerable. The clergy played a central role in community life and the Church was often the mediator in disputes and the provider of moral guidance.

PAUL RUBENS CELEBRATED CATHOLICISM THROUGH PAINTING

While the Spanish Netherlands remained under Habsburg control throughout the 17th century, the region faced several challenges, including economic decline and external threats. The loss of Antwerp as a major trading centre, combined with the continued dominance of the Dutch Republic in maritime trade, weakened the economy of the southern provinces. Additionally, the region was often caught in the crossfire of larger European conflicts, such as the Thirty Years' War and the Franco-Spanish War, both of which brought devastation and hardship to the Spanish Netherlands.

SUMMARY:

After the death of Charles the Bold, the Low Countries, including Belgium, passed to the Habsburg dynasty. In the early 16th century, Charles V, born in Ghent, became Holy Roman Emperor and ruled over a vast empire, including the Low Countries. Under his reign, the region faced growing tensions between Catholics and Protestants. His son, Philip II of Spain, attempted to impose Catholicism and centralised rule, leading to the Dutch Revolt in 1568. The northern provinces declared independence, while the southern provinces (modern-day Belgium) remained loyal to Spain and became the Spanish Netherlands. The Treaty of Westphalia (1648) confirmed this division and Belgium remained under Spanish control, marked by economic stagnation and religious repression.

✳ ✳ ✳

> **DID YOU KNOW?**
> The 1566 Beeldenstorm (Iconoclasm) saw widespread destruction of religious art and symbols across Belgium as part of a Protestant rebellion against Catholic Spain. This violent episode was part of the growing discontent in the Low Countries, leading to the Eighty Years' War and ultimately the separation of the Northern and Southern Netherlands.

PEOPLE:

Charles V (1500–1558) - Holy Roman Emperor, born in Ghent, ruled the Low Countries as part of his empire.
Philip II of Spain (1527–1598) - His policies triggered the Dutch Revolt.
Margaret of Parma (1522–1586) - Governor of the Netherlands under Philip II, attempted to enforce Catholicism.
Alba, Duke of (1507–1582) - Spanish general sent to suppress the Dutch Revolt, known for his harsh rule.

PLACES:

Brussels - Administrative capital of the Spanish Netherlands and later the Austrian Netherlands.
Antwerp - Major commercial city, severely impacted by the Dutch Revolt and the Sack of Antwerp (1576).
Ghent - A key city during the rebellion and under Habsburg control.
Leuven - A centre of Catholic learning during Spanish rule.

EVENTS:

Dutch Revolt (1568–1648) - Rebellion against Spanish rule in the Low Countries, resulting in the division between the independent Dutch Republic and the Spanish Netherlands.
Council of Troubles (1567–1573) - A court set up by the Duke of Alba to punish rebels, also known as the "Council of Blood."
Treaty of Westphalia (1648) - Ended the Thirty Years' War and formalised the division between the Dutch Republic and the Southern Netherlands.
Sack of Antwerp (1576) - Spanish troops mutinied, devastating the city and marking a turning point in the Revolt.

CHAPTER 5

AUSTRIAN AND FRENCH RULE

1713 - 1815

The 18th century was a period of significant transformation for Belgium, as it passed through two major foreign regimes: Austrian and French rule. During Austrian

THE FRENCH RULE IN BELGIUM FROM 1794 -1815

control, the region saw administrative and economic reforms influenced by Enlightenment ideas. However, the invasion of French revolutionary forces in the late 18th century radically altered Belgian society, bringing sweeping changes in law, governance and economy. The legacy of French occupation, particularly under Napoleonic rule, left a lasting impact on Belgian law, infrastructure and institutions, which continued to shape the country as it moved toward eventual independence in the 19th century.

Austrian Reforms and Enlightenment

The Austrian Habsburgs regained control of the southern Netherlands (present-day Belgium) following the Treaty of Utrecht in 1713, which ended the War of the Spanish Succession. The southern Netherlands became part of the Austrian Habsburg dominions and the region was governed from Vienna by the Austrian rulers, including Charles VI, Maria Theresa and Joseph II. Under Austrian rule, the southern Netherlands experienced a period of relative peace and stability, which allowed for the implementation of a series of administrative, economic and social reforms inspired by Enlightenment ideals.

Maria Theresa (reigned 1740-1780) and her son Joseph II (reigned 1780-1790) were key figures in introducing reforms to modernise the administration and improve the efficiency of governance in the Austrian Netherlands. One of the major initiatives was to reduce the power of local nobility and the Catholic Church, centralising authority under the Habsburg monarchy. This was part of a broader effort to streamline governance, reduce corruption and create a more uniform legal and administrative system across the Habsburg Empire. These reforms were in line with the Enlightenment ideals of rationalism, efficiency and state control.

Economically, the Austrians sought to modernise the southern Netherlands and encourage growth in trade and industry. The region was already a significant economic hub, with a thriving textile industry, but Austrian rulers made efforts to further develop its infrastructure and support industrial growth. Maria Theresa, in particular, promoted trade by improving roads, canals and ports, facilitating commerce and communication between the southern Netherlands and the rest of Europe. The construction of new roads and canals, such as the Brussels-Charleroi Canal, contributed to the economic integration of the region.

Joseph II's reign, however, marked a more radical phase of reform, which triggered significant resistance from various segments of society. Inspired by Enlightenment principles, Joseph II sought to reduce the influence of the Catholic Church in everyday life, instituting measures to limit the Church's control over education and religious institutions. He also introduced legal reforms, including the abolition of feudal privileges, the reform of the judiciary and the introduction of a new tax system aimed at promoting fairness and equality.

However, Joseph II's aggressive reform agenda, particularly his attempts to reduce the power of the Catholic Church and his centralising policies, sparked opposition among the nobility, clergy and common people in the southern Netherlands. The reforms threatened traditional privileges and local autonomy, leading to widespread discontent. This culminated in the Brabant Revolution of 1789-1790, a brief but significant rebellion against Austrian rule. Although the revolution was ultimately unsuccessful and Austrian control was restored, it revealed deep-seated tensions between the centralising tendencies of the Habsburgs and the desire for local autonomy in the southern Netherlands.

THE FRENCH REVOLUTIONARY IMPACT

The French Revolutionary Wars (1792-1802) brought about the most dramatic changes in the history of the southern Netherlands during the 18th century. In 1794, French revolutionary forces invaded the Austrian Netherlands and by 1795, the region was annexed by the French Republic, becoming part of France. This marked the end of Austrian rule and the beginning of a period of radical political, social and economic transformation under French control.

The French revolutionaries brought with them the ideas of liberty, equality and fraternity, as well as a desire to dismantle the old feudal structures and institutions that had governed the southern Netherlands for centuries. One of the most immediate impacts of French rule was the abolition of the feudal system. The French revolutionaries introduced sweeping reforms that abolished feudal privileges, titles and manorial rights, which had long been a source of power for the local nobility. In place of the old feudal order, the French established a more egalitarian system of governance, in which all citizens were theoretically equal before the law.

The French also dismantled the power of the Catholic Church, which had been one of the most influential institutions in Belgian society. Church lands were confiscated and sold, religious orders were disbanded and the Church was stripped of much of its wealth and influence. The French revolutionaries promoted secularism and sought to create a society free from religious influence. This led to considerable resistance in the largely Catholic southern Netherlands, where the population remained deeply attached to their faith.

Under French rule, the southern Netherlands was reorganised into departments, replacing the old provincial boundaries that had existed under Austrian rule. The French introduced a centralised administrative system, modelled on the French revolutionary government, which replaced the traditional local institutions. This reorganisation was part of a broader effort to integrate the southern Netherlands into the French state and to impose the French legal and administrative framework on the region.

In addition to political and social changes, the French revolutionaries also introduced significant economic reforms. The metric system, for example, was introduced during this period, replacing the complex array of local weights and measures that had previously existed. The French also attempted to modernise the economy by encouraging the growth of industry and commerce. However, the wars and economic disruptions caused by French occupation also led to hardship for many in the southern Netherlands, as trade was disrupted and resources were drained to support the French war effort.

LEGACY OF FRENCH OCCUPATION

The Napoleonic era (1799-1815) left a lasting legacy on the southern Netherlands, as many of the reforms introduced during French occupation continued to shape Belgian society long after the French left. Napoleon Bonaparte, who came to power in France in 1799, built on the reforms of the French Revolution, further centralising power and modernising the state. One of the most important legacies of Napoleonic rule was the introduction of the 'Code Napoléon', or the Napoleonic Civil Code, in 1804. This legal code replaced the patchwork of local laws and customs that had previously existed in the southern Netherlands with a uniform set of laws based on the principles of equality, property rights and individual liberty.

THE NAPOLEONIC CIVIL CODE OF 1804

The Napoleonic Civil Code laid the foundation for modern Belgian law and continues to influence the legal system in Belgium today. The code standardised laws across the region, ensuring that all citizens were subject to the same legal principles, regardless of their status or background. It also promoted the protection of private property, the legal equality of citizens and the secularisation of the legal system, which had previously been heavily influenced by the Catholic Church.

In addition to legal reforms, Napoleonic rule also had a profound impact on the economy and infrastructure of the southern Netherlands. Napoleon recognised the strategic importance of the region, particularly its proximity to the North Sea and its potential for economic growth. He invested in the development of infrastructure, including roads, canals and ports, to improve trade and communication. The construction of new roads and the modernisation of Antwerp's port during this period helped to lay the groundwork for Belgium's industrialisation in the 19th century.

Napoleon's economic policies also encouraged the growth of industry in the southern Netherlands. While the region had long been a centre of textile production, Napoleonic rule saw an expansion of industrial activity, particularly in coal mining and metalworking. These industries would become central to Belgium's economic development in the decades following independence.

However, Napoleonic rule was also marked by repression and military conscription, which caused considerable suffering among the population. Many Belgians were forced into the French army to fight in Napoleon's wars and the heavy taxation required to support the empire's military ambitions placed a strain on the economy. The defeat of Napoleon in 1815 at the Battle of Waterloo, located in present-day Belgium, brought an end to French control of the region and paved the way for the creation of the United Kingdom of the Netherlands, which included both Belgium and the Netherlands, under Dutch rule.

SUMMARY:

After the War of Spanish Succession (1701-1714), the Spanish Netherlands were ceded to the Austrian Habsburgs under the Treaty of Utrecht (1713). Austrian rule brought some reforms, particularly under Emperor Joseph II, but the region remained conservative and resistant to change. In 1794, during the French Revolutionary Wars, Belgium was annexed by France and integrated into the French Republic. French rule introduced significant changes, including the Napoleonic legal system and secularisation, but also brought heavy taxation and conscription, which were unpopular. After Napoleon's defeat at Waterloo in 1815, Belgium was merged with the Netherlands under the Congress of Vienna, forming the United Kingdom of the Netherlands.

DID YOU KNOW?

The Austrian Emperor Joseph II tried to modernise Belgium in the late 18th century by imposing Enlightenment reforms, which led to the short-lived Brabant Revolution of 1789. His attempts to reduce the power of the Catholic Church and reorganise government systems clashed with traditional Belgian values, sparking a rebellion that briefly established the United States of Belgium before being crushed.

PEOPLE:

Maria Theresa (1717–1780) - Austrian ruler who tried to modernise the Belgian provinces during the Austrian period.

Joseph II (1741–1790) - Introduced Enlightenment reforms, which were largely unpopular in the conservative Southern Netherlands.

Napoleon Bonaparte (1769–1821) - French Emperor who controlled Belgium from 1794 until his defeat in 1815.

Willem I (1772–1843) - King of the United Kingdom of the Netherlands after Napoleon's defeat.

PLACES:

Brussels - Continued as the political and cultural capital under Austrian rule.

Leuven - Its university was central to Catholic intellectual life, opposing Joseph II's reforms.

Waterloo - Site of Napoleon's final defeat in 1815.

EVENTS:

War of Spanish Succession (1701–1714) - Resulted in the transfer of Belgium to Austrian control.

Brabant Revolution (1789–1790) - A revolt against Austrian reforms, briefly establishing the United Belgian States.

French Revolutionary Wars (1794) - Belgium was annexed by the French Republic, marking the end of Austrian rule.

Battle of Waterloo (1815) - Napoleon's defeat near Brussels, leading to the Congress of Vienna, which merged Belgium with the Netherlands.

CHAPTER 6

THE BELGIAN REVOLUTION AND INDEPENDENCE

1830 - 1831

*T*he Belgian Revolution of 1830 was a defining moment in the history of Belgium, marking the country's emergence as an independent 

THE BELGIAN REVOLUTION OF 1830

state after years of Dutch rule. The revolution was fuelled by various causes, including deep-seated discontent over religious and linguistic tensions, economic grievances and the rise of Belgian nationalism. We visit key events leading to Belgium's independence and the establishment of a constitutional monarchy under King Leopold .

CAUSES OF REVOLUTION

The roots of the Belgian Revolution lay in the period following the defeat of Napoleon in 1815. The Congress of Vienna, which redrew the map of

Europe after the Napoleonic Wars, created the United Kingdom of the Netherlands, which united the northern Netherlands (modern-day Netherlands) and the southern Netherlands (modern-day Belgium) under the rule of King William I of the House of Orange. The intention was to create a strong, unified buffer state to prevent future French expansion. However, the union quickly became a source of tension, particularly for the southern provinces, which had a distinct cultural, linguistic and religious identity.

One of the primary causes of discontent was the deep divide between the Catholic, French-speaking population of the southern provinces (Belgium) and the Protestant, Dutch-speaking population of the northern Netherlands. The southern provinces had long been predominantly Catholic, while the north had a strong Protestant tradition. Under Dutch rule, King William I, a Protestant, sought to impose his authority by promoting Protestantism and limiting the influence of the Catholic Church in Belgium. This led to resentment among the Catholic population, who felt their religious rights were being infringed upon.

Language also became a major point of contention. The Dutch king attempted to impose Dutch as the official language in the southern provinces, despite the fact that French was the dominant language among the elites and urban classes in Belgium, while many in Flanders spoke regional dialects. The imposition of Dutch was seen as an attack on the cultural identity of the French-speaking Walloons and the elite classes, fuelling nationalist sentiment.

Economically, there was also a growing sense of inequality between the north and the south. While the northern Netherlands had a strong maritime and trading economy, the southern provinces were more industrialised, particularly in textiles and coal mining. The Belgians felt that the economic policies of King William I favoured the north and neglected the industrial interests of the south. The heavy taxation and economic centralisation further alienated many in the southern provinces, particularly the bourgeoisie, who became strong supporters of independence.

All these factors contributed to the rise of Belgian nationalism. Intellectuals, writers and politicians in the southern provinces began to articulate a distinct Belgian identity, emphasising their differences from the Dutch and their desire for greater autonomy. This growing nationalist sentiment created fertile ground for revolution.

THE REVOLUTION OF 1830

The spark for the Belgian Revolution came on 25 August 1830, during a performance of the opera 'La Muette de Portici' in Brussels. The opera, which tells the story of a popular revolt against foreign rule, resonated with the audience and by the end of the performance, crowds spilled into the streets, chanting nationalist slogans and demanding independence from Dutch rule. The spontaneous outbreak of unrest quickly escalated into a full-blown uprising, as riots and protests spread across Brussels and other major cities in the southern Netherlands.

In the following weeks, revolutionary fervour grew, with armed militias forming to resist Dutch forces. The revolutionaries were composed of a broad coalition of groups, including the Catholic clergy, who opposed the Protestant king, the French-speaking bourgeoisie, who resented Dutch linguistic policies and the working classes, who were suffering from economic hardship. This diverse coalition was united in its opposition to King William I's rule and its desire for an independent Belgian state.

Despite efforts by the Dutch government to suppress the uprising, the revolutionaries gained control of Brussels by September 1830. King William I sent troops to crush the rebellion, but they were met with fierce resistance. After several days of intense fighting, known as the "September Days," the Dutch forces were forced to withdraw from Brussels. The victory of the revolutionaries in Brussels marked a turning point in the revolution and by the end of September, most of the southern provinces were under the control of the Belgian rebels.

On 4 October 1830, the provisional Belgian government declared independence from the Netherlands, formally breaking away from Dutch rule. The declaration of independence was a bold move, but the revolutionaries were determined to create a new state free from the control of the Dutch crown. The Belgian revolutionaries also sought international recognition and support for their cause, appealing to the great powers of Europe to legitimise their independence.

AN ARTIST'S DEPICTION OF THE BELGIAN REVOLUTION IN BRUSSELS

THE CONSTITUTIONAL MONARCHY

In the aftermath of the revolution, the newly formed Belgian state faced the challenge of creating a stable government that could unite the diverse factions that had participated in the revolution. The solution came in the form of a constitutional monarchy, a system of government that would balance the power of the monarchy with the principles of representative government. The decision to establish a monarchy was influenced by the need to gain the support of the European powers, who were wary of revolutionary republics but more inclined to support a stable, constitutional monarchy.

In February 1831, the Belgian National Congress, which had been convened to draft a constitution, offered the throne to Leopold of Saxe-Coburg and Gotha, a German prince who had connections to several European royal families. Leopold, who was known for his diplomatic skills and moderate politics, accepted the offer and was crowned King Leopold

I of Belgium on 21 July 1831. This day, which marks the beginning of Leopold's reign, is still celebrated as Belgium's national day.

LEOPOLD I OF SAXE-COBURG FIRST KING OF THE BELGIANS

The Belgian Constitution, adopted in 1831, was one of the most liberal constitutions of its time. It established Belgium as a constitutional monarchy with a parliamentary system of government. The constitution guaranteed fundamental rights and freedoms, including freedom of religion, freedom of the press and freedom of assembly. It also established the separation of powers, with an elected parliament and an independent judiciary. The Catholic Church retained a strong influence in Belgian society, but the constitution ensured religious freedom for all citizens.

The Belgian political system was designed to accommodate the country's linguistic and religious diversity. Although French remained the dominant language in government and the judiciary, the constitution recognised the rights of Dutch speakers and allowed for the use of Dutch in certain regions. This framework laid the foundation for the later development of Belgium's complex system of linguistic and regional autonomy.

Internationally, the Belgian Revolution posed a challenge to the European powers, who had agreed at the Congress of Vienna to maintain the territorial status quo. However, after initial hesitation, the major powers, including France, Britain and Austria, eventually recognised Belgian independence. The Treaty of London, signed in 1839, formalised Belgium's independence and established its borders, which remain largely the same today.

SUMMARY:

Unrest grew in Belgium under Dutch rule, driven by religious, linguistic and economic disparities. The Dutch were predominantly Protestant, while Belgium was largely Catholic. Additionally, Dutch efforts to impose the Dutch language in administration angered the French-speaking elite in Belgium. In 1830, sparked by a performance of the patriotic opera "La Muette de Portici" in Brussels, protests erupted, leading to a full-scale revolution. After several months of fighting, Belgium declared independence and in 1831, Leopold I of Saxe-Coburg was crowned the first King of the Belgians. The country's independence was guaranteed by the Treaty of London (1839), which declared Belgium a neutral state.

DID YOU KNOW?

Belgium's national anthem, "La Brabançonne," was hastily written in 1830 during the revolutionary fervor that led to Belgium's independence. The anthem reflects the patriotic zeal of the time, celebrating the fight for freedom from Dutch rule, with lyrics initially calling for King William I's expulsion.

PEOPLE:

Leopold I (1790–1865) - Belgium's first king, who established the country's constitutional monarchy.

Charles Rogier (1800–1885) - Revolutionary leader and later prime minister who helped organise Belgium's independence.

Étienne Constantin de Gerlache (1785–1871) - First President of the Belgian Chamber of Representatives and an important figure in the Belgian Revolution.

PLACES:

Brussels - The main stage for the 1830 Belgian Revolution, leading to independence.

Liège - A major industrial city, also a hotbed of revolutionary activity.

London - The city where the Treaty of London (1839) was signed, securing Belgium's independence.

EVENTS:

Belgian Revolution (1830) - Uprising against Dutch rule, sparked by opera performances and nationalist sentiments.

Coronation of Leopold I (1831) - Leopold I became the first King of the Belgians, cementing the nation's independence.

Treaty of London (1839) - Recognised Belgium's independence and guaranteed its neutrality.

CHAPTER 7

THE INDUSTRIAL REVOLUTION

c. 1830 - 1900

*T*he period from 1850 to 1900 was a time of profound transformation in Belgium, as the country experienced the full impact of the Industrial Revolution.

THE INDUSTRIAL REVOLUTION

Economic growth, fuelled by advancements in coal mining, textiles and steel production, led to rapid urbanisation and the emergence of a new social order. The rise of a working class, coupled with poor living conditions, gave birth to organised labour movements and class struggle. These tensions, along with growing political awareness, eventually spurred social and political reforms, including the extension of voting rights and the introduction of labour protections. This section will view the economic, social and political changes that reshaped Belgium during this transformative period.

ECONOMIC TRANSFORMATION AND URBANISATION

The mid-19th century marked the acceleration of Belgium's Industrial Revolution, which had begun earlier in the century. Belgium, as one of the first countries on the European continent to industrialise, became a leading industrial power, with significant advancements in key sectors such as coal mining, textiles and steel production. The availability of natural resources, especially coal in regions like Wallonia, provided the necessary energy to power factories, railways and the burgeoning manufacturing industry.

Coal mining was at the heart of Belgium's industrial expansion, with the southern provinces, particularly the Sillon Industriel (the Industrial Belt), becoming the hub of mining activity. By the late 19th century, Belgium had developed an extensive railway network, further facilitating the transportation of coal and other goods. The railway system not only connected major industrial centres such as Liège and Charleroi with the rest of Europe but also spurred the growth of new industries. This included steel production, with companies like Cockerill in Liège playing a pivotal role in making Belgium one of the world's leading steel producers.

Textile manufacturing, particularly in Flanders, also contributed to Belgium's industrialisation. While the region had a long tradition of textile production, industrial machinery allowed for increased productivity, leading to the expansion of textile factories in cities like Ghent. As factories replaced traditional artisanal production methods, more people moved to cities in search of work, resulting in rapid urbanisation.

The migration of workers from rural areas to industrial cities led to the dramatic growth of urban centres. Between 1850 and 1900, cities like Brussels, Antwerp and Liège saw their populations swell, transforming Belgium into one of the most urbanised countries in Europe. However, this urban expansion was often unplanned and the rapid influx of workers created overcrowded and unsanitary living conditions, particularly in working-class neighbourhoods.

TYPICAL SCENE FROM AN INDUSTRIAL SITE IN BELGIUM

CLASS STRUGGLE AND EARLY LABOUR MOVEMENTS

The Industrial Revolution brought about significant changes in the structure of Belgian society, particularly with the emergence of a large working class. The rapid expansion of factories and mines created demand for labour, drawing men, women and even children into harsh working environments. For many workers, life in the newly industrialised cities was marked by long hours, low wages and dangerous working conditions. Child labour was widespread and there were few legal protections for workers in terms of safety or rights.

THE BELGIAN WORKERS' (POB) WAS FOUNDED IN 1885

The stark contrast between the wealth of industrialists and the poverty of the working class led to growing social tensions. By the mid-19th century, class consciousness among workers began to take root, as they became increasingly aware of their collective grievances. Early labour movements began to form, with workers organising to demand better wages, improved working conditions and shorter working hours. However, the Belgian government, which was dominated by the conservative and wealthy elite, was initially hostile to these movements, often suppressing strikes and protests.

The situation for workers was exacerbated by the economic crises of the 1870s, which led to widespread unemployment and further impoverishment of the working class. In response to these conditions, socialist ideologies began to gain traction among the Belgian proletariat. In 1885, the Belgian Workers' Party (Parti Ouvrier Belge, POB) was founded, becoming the country's first organised socialist party. The POB played a key role in mobilising workers, advocating for social reforms and pushing for political change.

One of the most significant expressions of worker discontent during this period was the general strike of 1886, which saw widespread protests and violent confrontations between workers and the authorities. The strike, which began in the industrial regions of Wallonia, was fuelled by economic hardship and the demand for better working conditions. The government's brutal repression of the strike highlighted the deep social divisions in Belgian society, but it also drew attention to the need for reform.

SOCIAL REFORMS AND POLITICAL CHANGES

The growing unrest among the working class, combined with pressure from emerging socialist movements, eventually forced the Belgian government to introduce social reforms. Throughout the late 19th century, Belgium began to slowly address some of the worst abuses of industrial labour, particularly child labour and working conditions. One of the key milestones was the passage of legislation in 1889 that limited the working hours of women and children, marking the first step towards improving labour rights in the country.

However, the demand for political change was just as pressing as the call for social reforms. At the beginning of the 19th century, Belgium's political system was highly restrictive, with voting rights limited to wealthy male property owners. This exclusionary system prevented the majority of the population, particularly the working class, from participating in the political process. The extension of suffrage became a central demand of the labour movement, with socialists, liberals and even some Catholic reformers pushing for more democratic participation.

The pressure for political reform culminated in the introduction of partial universal male suffrage in 1893. This reform allowed all men over the age of 25 to vote, although wealthier citizens retained additional voting power through a system of plural voting, which granted them more votes based on property ownership or education. Despite this limitation, the 1893 electoral reform was a significant victory for the working class and marked the beginning of the democratisation of Belgian politics.

The extension of voting rights led to increased representation of socialist and progressive parties in the Belgian parliament, allowing for further social and labour reforms. In the closing years of the 19th century, Belgium began to introduce measures aimed at improving working conditions, such as the establishment of labour inspection services and the legal recognition of trade unions. These reforms, while limited, laid the groundwork for the more comprehensive welfare state that would develop in the 20th century.

SUMMARY:

Belgium was the first country in continental Europe to undergo industrialisation, starting in the early 19th century. The Sillon industriel (Industrial Valley) in Wallonia became the centre of coal mining and steel production. The textile industry also expanded rapidly in Flanders. Industrialisation transformed the economy and society, leading to urbanisation, the rise of a working class and significant social changes. By the late 19th century, Belgium saw the rise of socialist and workers' movements advocating for improved labour conditions. The general strike of 1893 led to the introduction of universal male suffrage (though initially limited). Politically, Belgium became increasingly divided along linguistic and economic lines.

DID YOU KNOW?

By the late 19th century, Belgium was the second most industrialised nation in the world, after the United Kingdom. Belgium's rich coal reserves, iron production, and textile industries fuelled this rapid industrialisation, particularly in cities like Liège and Charleroi, drastically transforming the country's social fabric.

PEOPLE:

John Cockerill (1790–1840) - Industrialist who played a key role in Belgium's industrialisation, especially in ironworks.

Emile Vandervelde (1866–1938) - Prominent socialist leader and advocate for workers' rights.

André Dumont (1847–1920) - Geologist who discovered coal in Limburg, crucial for Belgium's industrial growth.

PLACES:

Sillon industriel - The industrial valley in Wallonia, a key centre for coal mining and steel production.

Charleroi - Became a major industrial city, particularly in coal and steel.

Liège - Also an important industrial centre, especially in steel and engineering.

EVENTS:

Belgium's Industrial Boom (1850–1900) - Belgium became the first continental European country to industrialise, especially in coal, steel and textiles.

General Strike of 1893 - Led to political reforms, including the introduction of universal male suffrage.

Formation of the Belgian Workers' Party (1885) - First socialist party in Belgium, advocating for labour rights.

CHAPTER 8

BELGIUM IN THE WORLD WARS

1914 – 1945

*T*he two World Wars had a profound and lasting impact on Belgium, a country that found itself on the frontlines of both global conflicts. During World War I, Belgium suffered greatly after its invasion by Germany, an event that became infamous as

WWI BELGIAN SOLDIERS AT THE FRONT IN 1914

the "Rape of Belgium" due to the brutal treatment of its civilian population and the devastation of its towns and cities. In the interwar years, Belgium focused on recovery and maintaining a policy of neutrality, although political tensions in Europe continued to rise. The outbreak of World War II saw Belgium once again invaded and occupied by German forces, leading to widespread suffering, resistance, collaboration and eventual liberation by the Allies. This chapter will reveal Belgium's experience during both World Wars, its efforts to recover *during the interwar period and the lasting consequences of these conflicts.*

WORLD WAR I: THE RAPE OF BELGIUM

At the outbreak of World War I in 1914, Belgium's strategic location between France and Germany made it a central focus in Germany's war plans. Under the Schlieffen Plan, the German army sought to quickly defeat France by moving through neutral Belgium, despite the latter's established policy of neutrality. On 4 August 1914, Germany invaded Belgium after King Albert I refused to grant free passage to German troops. The invasion marked the beginning of a brutal occupation that would last for much of the war.

The German invasion was accompanied by widespread atrocities against Belgian civilians, leading to what became known as the "Rape of Belgium." German forces, frustrated by unexpected Belgian resistance, resorted to violent reprisals against the civilian population, burning towns and executing civilians. Cities like Leuven (Louvain), known for its historic university, were particularly hard-hit, with significant cultural and architectural heritage destroyed. Reports of German atrocities, including massacres and the deliberate targeting of civilians, shocked the international community and were used as propaganda by the Allies to galvanise public opinion against Germany.

Despite the overwhelming force of the German military, Belgium offered unexpected and fierce resistance. Under the leadership of King Albert I, the Belgian army slowed the German advance, particularly at the Battle of Liège, where the city's fortifications held out longer than expected. Although the Belgian forces were eventually overwhelmed, the delay caused by their resistance allowed the French and British armies to mobilise and counter the German offensive.

For the duration of the war, Belgium was divided into two zones: the majority of the country was occupied by German forces, while the remaining Belgian army, along with King Albert I, retreated to a small corner of unoccupied territory in the west, near Ypres. The Belgian population under occupation endured severe hardship, with food shortages, forced labour and repression becoming a daily reality. Belgian resistance movements emerged, but the German occupiers responded with harsh measures, including deportations and executions.

Belgium's suffering during World War I became a symbol of the brutality of modern warfare and played a key role in shaping international sympathy for the country. By the end of the war in 1918, much of Belgium lay in ruins, with its infrastructure, economy and cities devastated.

BELGIUM'S SUFFERING DURING WORLD WAR I

INTERWAR RECOVERY AND NEUTRALITY

In the aftermath of World War I, Belgium faced the enormous challenge of rebuilding a country that had been severely damaged by the war. The Treaty of Versailles, signed in 1919, provided some compensation for Belgium's losses, including reparations from Germany, but the scale of destruction was immense. Towns and cities needed to be rebuilt, agriculture and industry had to be restored and large parts of the population were displaced. Belgium also regained control of the Eupen-Malmedy region, which had been ceded to Germany following the Franco-Prussian War, further solidifying its borders.

The Belgian government, under the leadership of King Albert I, implemented policies to aid in the recovery process, focusing on infrastructure, industry and the housing of the population. Despite the enormous cost of rebuilding, Belgium was able to recover relatively quickly, thanks in part to its industrial base, which resumed production by the early 1920s.

In foreign policy, Belgium returned to its pre-war policy of neutrality, seeking to avoid entanglement in the growing tensions between European powers. The horrors of World War I left a deep impression on the Belgian population and the government was determined to prevent another conflict on Belgian soil. However, Belgium's policy of neutrality was increasingly difficult to maintain in the face of the rise of fascism in Germany and Italy and growing tensions across Europe.

Politically, the interwar years were also a period of rising internal tensions. The economic difficulties of the Great Depression in the 1930s, combined with the spread of fascist and communist ideologies across Europe, led to increased political polarisation within Belgium. Far-right and far-left movements gained traction, contributing to social unrest. However, despite these challenges, Belgium remained committed to its neutral stance, even as the international situation deteriorated.

WORLD WAR II: OCCUPATION AND LIBERATION

Belgium's commitment to neutrality was tested once again in 1940, when Nazi Germany launched its Blitzkrieg offensive across Western Europe. On 10 May 1940, German forces invaded Belgium, bypassing the heavily fortified French Maginot Line. Despite efforts by the Belgian army and the support of British and French forces, the Germans quickly overwhelmed Belgium's defences. King Leopold III surrendered to the Germans on 28 May 1940, a controversial decision that led to divisions within the Belgian government and accusations of collaboration.

GERMAN RIDERS AND MOTORCYCLISTS IN FRANCE IN 1940

The German occupation of Belgium during World War II was marked by widespread repression, economic exploitation and suffering. The Nazi regime imposed strict control over the country, suppressing political dissent and implementing anti-Jewish measures. Thousands of Belgian Jews were deported to concentration camps and the country's resources were exploited to support the German war effort. Forced labour became widespread, with many Belgians compelled to work in German factories or in support of the occupying army.

Despite the harsh conditions of occupation, resistance movements began to emerge across Belgium. Groups like the 'Armée Secrète' and the 'Front de l'Indépendance' engaged in acts of sabotage, espionage and the protection of Jewish citizens. The Belgian resistance, although fragmented, played a significant role in undermining the German occupation and many Belgians risked their lives to assist the Allies.

Collaboration was also a reality during the occupation, with some Belgians, particularly those aligned with far-right groups like the 'Rex' party, cooperating with the Nazi regime. These collaborators were often involved in the administration of the occupation or in assisting the Gestapo in identifying resistance members. After the war, many collaborators were tried and punished, though the question of collaboration remained a sensitive issue in post-war Belgian society.

Belgium's liberation came as Allied forces advanced through Western Europe following the Normandy landings in June 1944. In September 1944, Brussels and Antwerp were liberated by British and American forces and by early 1945, the country was free from German occupation. The port of Antwerp played a crucial role in the Allied war effort, serving as a key supply hub for the final push into Germany.

The aftermath of the Second World War was a period of reckoning for Belgium. The issue of King Leopold III's conduct during the war and his surrender to the Germans remained highly controversial, leading to the so-called "Royal Question" and his eventual abdication in 1951. Belgium also faced the challenges of post-war reconstruction, with much of the country's infrastructure once again devastated by conflict. However, unlike the First World War, Belgium emerged from the Second World War with stronger international ties, particularly through its involvement in the establishment of NATO and the European Economic Community, laying the foundation for its future role in European integration.

The period following the Second World War was a significant time of reflection and decision-making for Belgium. The controversy surrounding King Leopold III's actions during the war, especially his decision to surrender to the Germans, sparked intense debate and led to what became known as the "Royal Question." This controversy ultimately resulted in King Leopold III abdicating the throne in 1951. In addition to dealing with this political turmoil, Belgium had to address the extensive damage to its infrastructure caused by the war.

The task of rebuilding the nation was formidable, as much of the country had been ravaged by the conflict. Despite these challenges, Belgium's post-war period was marked by a strengthening of its international relationships. Unlike the aftermath of the First World War, Belgium emerged from the Second World War with a more robust network of international alliances. This was exemplified by its active participation in the founding of NATO and the European Economic Community. These developments were crucial in establishing Belgium's future role in the process of European integration, setting the stage for its involvement in the broader European project.

SUMMARY:

Belgium's neutrality was violated by Germany in both World Wars. In 1914, Germany invaded Belgium as part of the Schlieffen Plan, leading to widespread destruction, including the burning of Leuven. Belgium became a symbol of Allied resistance and after the war, it was rewarded with the small territories of Eupen and Malmedy. In World War II, Belgium was again invaded by Nazi Germany in 1940 and occupied until 1944. King Leopold III's controversial decision to surrender led to a post-war crisis. The Belgian Resistance played a significant role in undermining German occupation.

DID YOU KNOW?

The term "sneak attack" originates partly from the German invasion of Belgium in World War I, when the neutral nation was unexpectedly overrun as part of the Schlieffen Plan in 1914. Despite its neutrality, Belgium became the battleground for both World Wars, enduring significant destruction and military occupation, which forever shaped its national identity.

PEOPLE:

King Albert I (1875–1934) - Led Belgian resistance against the German invasion during World War I.

King Leopold III (1901–1983) - Controversially surrendered to Nazi Germany in World War II, leading to post- war political issues.

Paul- Henri Spaak (1899–1972) - Prime Minister during and after WWII, later a leading figure in European integration.

PLACES:

Ypres - Site of numerous World War I battles, including the use of chemical weapons.

Bastogne - Key battleground during the Battle of the Bulge (1944–1945) in WWII.

Liège - A fortified city that saw early fighting during both World Wars.

EVENTS:

German Invasion of Belgium (1914) - Led to brutal occupation during World War I, violating Belgium's neutrality.

Battle of Ypres (1914–1917) - A series of WWI battles in Flanders, known for heavy casualties and the use of gas warfare.

German Occupation (1940–1944) - Belgium was occupied during World War II until its liberation by the Allies in 1944.

CHAPTER 9

POST-WAR RECOVERY AND EUROPEAN INTEGRATION

1945-1993

In the aftermath of World War II, Belgium faced the monumental task of rebuilding its economy and infrastructure, much of which had been severely damaged

EUROPEAN INTERGRATION BEGINS

by the war. Despite the devastation, Belgium was quick to recover, aided by strategic economic policies and international assistance, such as the Marshall Plan. During this period, Belgium played a pioneering role in the early stages of European integration, contributing to the formation of the European Coal and Steel Community (ECSC), a precursor to the European Union (EU). Brussels soon emerged as a political hub for Europe, eventually becoming home to key EU institutions and NATO headquarters. Belgium's post-war recovery, its role in the birth of the European Union and the rise of Brussels as the de facto capital of Europe will be examined.

RECONSTRUCTION AND ECONOMIC RECOVERY

Belgium's post-war recovery was shaped by a combination of domestic policies and international support, most notably through the Marshall Plan. As part of the broader European recovery effort, Belgium received substantial financial aid from the United States to rebuild its infrastructure and revitalise its economy. The funds were used to repair roads, railways and industrial facilities that had been damaged during the war, as well as to modernise factories and increase productivity. The Belgian government, led by the Christian Social Party (Parti Social Chrétien), took an active role in directing reconstruction efforts and fostering economic growth.

By the early 1950s, Belgium had made significant progress in rebuilding its economy. Industrial output increased, particularly in key sectors such as coal mining, steel production and manufacturing. The coal-rich region of Wallonia, which had been central to Belgium's industrialisation in the 19th century, continued to play an important role in the country's economic recovery. At the same time, the port of Antwerp, one of Europe's largest, became a major hub for international trade, further boosting Belgium's economic standing.

However, the post-war period also saw the beginning of economic and social shifts within Belgium. Flanders, which had traditionally been more agricultural, began to industrialise rapidly, with the growth of sectors such as textiles and chemicals. This shift marked the start of a gradual economic realignment, as Flanders began to outpace Wallonia in terms of growth and development. This north-south divide would later have political ramifications, contributing to the rise of regionalist movements in the second half of the 20th century.

STREET VIEW OF BRUSSELS IN 1950

Socially, Belgium implemented a range of welfare reforms in the post-war years, including the expansion of social security systems, unemployment benefits and healthcare services. These reforms were aimed at improving living standards for the working class and reducing the inequalities exacerbated by the war. The Belgian government also focused on education, expanding access to schooling and promoting technical and vocational training to meet the demands of the modernising economy.

THE BIRTH OF THE EUROPEAN UNION

Belgium's post-war recovery coincided with a growing desire for European integration, driven by the belief that economic cooperation would prevent future conflicts. Belgium was a leading proponent of this vision, recognising that closer ties between European countries could promote peace, stability and economic prosperity. As one of the six founding members of the European Coal and Steel Community (ECSC), Belgium played a key role in the creation of what would eventually become the European Union.

The ECSC, established in 1951, aimed to integrate the coal and steel industries of its member states—Belgium, France, West Germany, Italy, Luxembourg and the Netherlands—under a supranational authority. For Belgium, whose economy relied heavily on coal and steel, participation in the ECSC offered an opportunity to stabilise its industries and strengthen its ties with neighbouring countries. The success of the ECSC demonstrated the potential of European economic cooperation and paved the way for further integration.

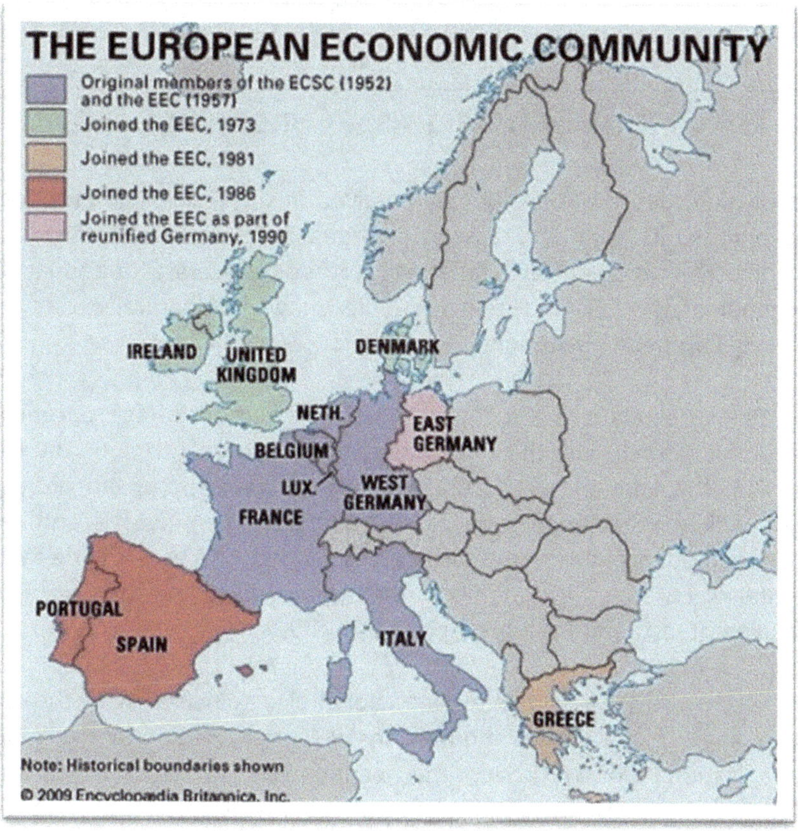

ECSC MAP: BELGIUM WAS ONE OF THE ORIGINAL MEMBERS IN 1951

Building on the ECSC's achievements, Belgium continued to advocate for deeper European unity. In 1957, Belgium, along with the other ECSC members, signed the Treaty of Rome, which established the European Economic Community (EEC). The EEC marked a significant step toward the creation of a common market, with the goal of eliminating trade barriers and promoting economic integration across Europe. Belgium's commitment to the EEC reflected its belief in the benefits of a united Europe and its strategic position at the heart of the continent.

The success of these early integration efforts laid the foundation for the European Union as it exists today. Belgium's role in these initiatives earned it a reputation as one of the most committed supporters of European integration and its leadership in the process cemented its position within the emerging European order.

THE RISE OF BRUSSELS AS A EUROPEAN CAPITAL

As Belgium became more deeply involved in the process of European integration, its capital, Brussels, emerged as the political centre of Europe. The city's central location, its status as the capital of a founding member of the EEC and its accessibility made it a natural choice for hosting European institutions.

In 1958, Brussels was selected as the headquarters of the European Economic Community, the forerunner to the European Union. The city became the administrative centre for the growing European project, hosting key institutions such as the European Commission and the European Council. Over time, Brussels expanded its role as the de facto capital of Europe, with additional institutions, including the European Parliament, establishing a presence in the city.

The rise of Brussels as a European capital also coincided with the city becoming a major diplomatic hub. In 1967, the North Atlantic Treaty Organisation (NATO) moved its headquarters to Brussels, further elevating the city's international profile. The presence of both EU institutions and NATO transformed Brussels into a political and diplomatic centre, attracting policymakers, diplomats and international organisations from around the world.

The growth of Brussels as a political capital brought both benefits and challenges to Belgium. On the one hand, it cemented Belgium's position at the heart of European and transatlantic decision-making, enhancing its international influence. On the other hand, the influx of international organisations and expatriates placed strain on the city's infrastructure, leading to challenges related to housing, transport and governance.

SUMMARY:

After WWII, Belgium quickly recovered with the help of the Marshall Plan. The country played a pivotal role in founding international organisations, including NATO (with headquarters in Brussels) and the European Economic Community (EEC) in 1957, the precursor to the European Union. Belgium's capital, Brussels, became the de facto capital of the EU. The post-war period also saw the end of Belgium's colonial empire, with the independence of Congo in 1960, which marked a difficult and violent decolonisation process.

DID YOU KNOW?

Belgium was one of the founding members of the European Coal and Steel Community in 1951, the precursor to the European Union. This marked the beginning of Belgium's pivotal role in European integration, as the ECSC's headquarters was based in Brussels, which would later become the de facto capital of the EU.

PEOPLE:

Paul- Henri Spaak (1899–1972) - One of the founding fathers of the European Union and NATO.

King Baudouin (1930–1993) - King of Belgium during much of the post-war period, symbol of national unity.

Leopold III - Abdicated in 1951 after controversy over his actions during WWII.

PLACES:

Brussels - Emerged as the de facto capital of Europe, home to the European Commission and NATO.

Congo - Belgian colony that gained independence in 1960, marking the end of Belgium's colonial empire.

EVENTS:

Independence of Congo (1960) - Marked the end of Belgian colonialism.

Formation of the European Economic Community (1957) - Belgium was a founding member, contributing to European integration.

NATO Headquarters (1967) - Brussels became the headquarters of NATO, reflecting Belgium's central role in post- war diplomacy.

CHAPTER 10

FEDERALISM AND REGIONALISM

1970 - 2000

THE BELGIAN PARLIAMENT IN BRUSSELS

During the latter half of the 20th century, Belgium underwent profound political, cultural and social transformations driven by deepening regionalism and linguistic divides between its two main communities: the Dutch-speaking Flemish in the north and the French-speaking Walloons in the south. These tensions led to a significant reconfiguration of the Belgian state, shifting from a centralised unitary structure to a federal system that granted increasing autonomy to the regions. This following section explores the growing linguistic divide between Flanders and Wallonia, the process of devolution that culminated in the creation of a federal state and how these changes reshaped Belgian politics, culture and national identity.

LANGUAGE AND IDENTITY: FLEMISH AND WALLOON DIVIDE

The roots of the linguistic divide in Belgium stretch back to the country's formation in 1830, but it was in the post-World War II era that these differences became a focal point of political conflict. Belgium is home to two main linguistic communities: the Flemish, who speak Dutch (Flemish) and the Walloons, who speak French. A small German-speaking community also resides in the east. Historically, French had been the dominant language of government, business and culture, even in Flanders, where the majority of the population spoke Dutch. This linguistic imbalance fostered resentment among the Flemish, who felt that their language and culture were being marginalised.

By the 1960s, tensions between the Flemish and Walloon communities were exacerbated by economic disparities. Flanders, which had traditionally been more rural and less developed, began to experience rapid industrialisation and economic growth, while Wallonia, historically the industrial heartland of Belgium due to its coal and steel industries, entered a period of decline. As Flanders' economic power increased, so did calls for greater recognition of its linguistic and cultural identity.

The linguistic divide became institutionalised through a series of language laws and reforms aimed at recognising the distinctiveness of Belgium's communities. In 1962, Belgium established official language borders, dividing the country into Dutch-speaking Flanders, French-speaking Wallonia and the bilingual Brussels-Capital Region. These reforms were intended to protect linguistic rights and ease tensions, but in practice, they highlighted the deepening divide between the two regions. Language and identity became central to Belgian politics, with parties increasingly aligning along linguistic lines.

DEVOLUTION AND THE FEDERAL STATE

As regional identities grew stronger, pressure mounted for political reform that would give greater autonomy to Flanders, Wallonia and the Brussels-Capital Region. In response, Belgium embarked on a series of state reforms, beginning in the 1970s, that gradually transformed the country from a unitary state to a federal one.

The first major step towards devolution came in 1970 with the constitutional reform that recognised Belgium's three linguistic communities (Dutch-speaking, French-speaking and German-speaking) and three regions (Flanders, Wallonia and Brussels). This laid the groundwork for further decentralisation of power. Over the next two decades, Belgium's political structure evolved through a series of constitutional reforms, each granting more autonomy to the regions and communities.

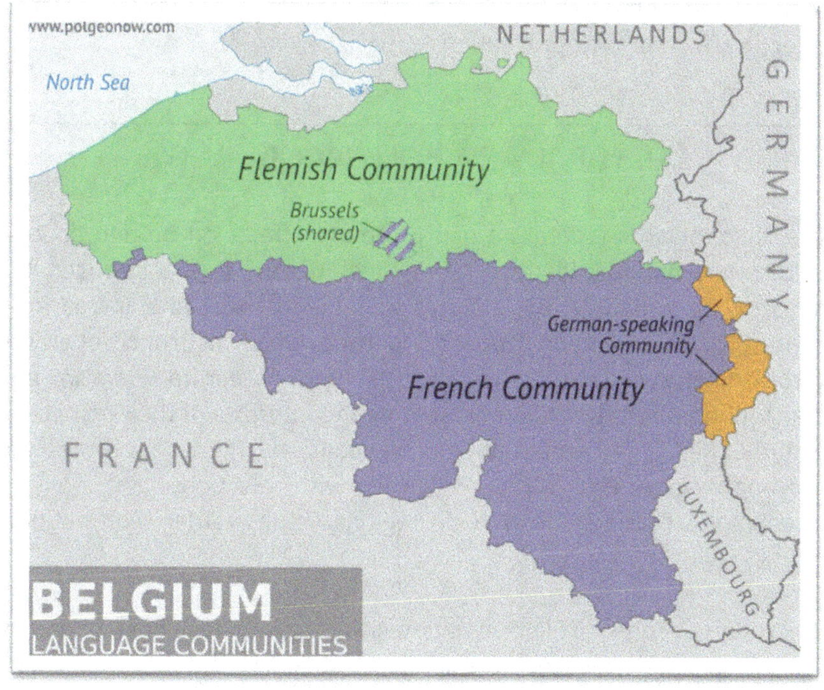

MAP OF THE REGIONAL LANGUAGES IN BELGIUM

The state reforms of 1980 were particularly significant, as they created regional governments for Flanders and Wallonia, each with its own parliament and executive authority. The Brussels-Capital Region, due to its bilingual nature and political sensitivity, received its own regional government in 1989. These reforms marked the formalisation of

Belgium's federal structure, with powers over areas such as education, culture and regional economic policy being devolved to the regions and communities.

The devolution process reached its culmination with the 1993 constitutional reform, which officially declared Belgium a federal state. This reform further clarified the division of powers between the federal government and the regions and communities. The regions were granted significant control over economic, transport and environmental policies, while the communities were responsible for areas related to language, culture and education. The federal government retained authority over national defence, foreign policy and justice, among other areas, but the regions and communities gained considerable autonomy in matters directly affecting their populations.

CULTURAL AND POLITICAL CHANGES

The shift towards federalism had profound effects on Belgian politics, culture and national identity. As regional identities grew stronger, the concept of a unified Belgian national identity became increasingly contested. The traditional political parties, which had once operated across linguistic lines, gradually split into separate Flemish and Francophone parties, each representing the interests of their respective communities. This fragmentation of the political landscape reflected the growing regionalism within Belgium, with elections and political discourse increasingly centred on regional issues rather than national ones.

In Flanders, a sense of Flemish nationalism began to take hold, driven by both linguistic pride and economic confidence. Flemish nationalist parties, such as the Volksunie and later the New Flemish Alliance (N-VA), gained traction by advocating for greater autonomy for Flanders, with some even calling for full independence. Flemish nationalists argued that Flanders, with its booming economy, should not have to subsidise the poorer Wallonia and that further devolution was necessary to protect Flemish interests.

In Wallonia, the decline of traditional industries and the economic difficulties of the post-war period led to different political dynamics. Walloon political leaders focused on securing economic support and investment from the federal government, while advocating for greater autonomy to address the region's specific economic challenges. Walloon identity, while strong, did not develop the same nationalist overtones as in Flanders, but regional pride remained an important part of political life.

The Brussels-Capital Region, as a bilingual and multicultural city, developed its own unique political identity. Brussels became not only the capital of Belgium but also the capital of the European Union, with the city's international character influencing its politics and culture. The presence of EU institutions and international organisations in Brussels created a cosmopolitan atmosphere, setting it apart from the more regionally focused politics of Flanders and Wallonia.

As regionalism grew, so did debates about the future of Belgium as a unified state. While federalism allowed for greater regional autonomy, it also raised questions about how much further the process of decentralisation could go without threatening the existence of the Belgian state. These debates often centred on economic issues, with Flanders pushing for more fiscal autonomy and Wallonia seeking continued federal support.

Despite these challenges, federalism allowed Belgium to navigate its linguistic and regional divides relatively peacefully. The country's political system adapted to accommodate the growing regionalism and while tensions remained, Belgium avoided the violent conflicts that characterised other divided states. The Belgian model of federalism became an example of how a deeply divided society could manage its differences through political compromise and decentralisation.

SUMMARY:

Starting in the 1970s, tensions between the Dutch-speaking Flemings in the north and French-speaking Walloons in the south led to constitutional reforms, transforming Belgium into a federal state. Major reforms in 1970, 1980, 1988-89 and 1993 granted greater autonomy to the regions of Flanders, Wallonia and the Brussels-Capital Region. Linguistic and cultural divisions remain significant in Belgian politics, with regular political crises reflecting regional and linguistic disagreements.

DID YOU KNOW?

Belgium's complex linguistic divide has led to the country having six different governments. The growing regionalism in Belgium led to a federal state system in 1993, with governments for the Flemish, Walloon, Brussels, and three language communities, reflecting the cultural and political divisions in the country.

KEY PEOPLE, PLACES AND EVENTS OF THE ERA

PEOPLE:

King Baudouin (1930–1993) - Symbol of national unity during a period of increasing regionalism.

Bart De Wever (b. 1970) - Leader of the New Flemish Alliance, advocating for Flemish autonomy.

Elio Di Rupo (b. 1951) - Belgian politician, Walloon socialist and former Prime Minister during a period of complex coalition governments.

PLACES:

Flanders - The Dutch- speaking northern region, economically more dynamic, advocating for more autonomy.

Wallonia - The French- speaking southern region, economically weaker than Flanders.

Brussels - Officially bilingual, but a major point of contention between Flemish and Francophone communities.

EVENTS:

State Reforms (1970–1993) - Belgium transitioned into a federal state with devolved powers to regions and language communities.

Political Crises (2007–2011) - Belgium faced long government formation periods due to linguistic and political divides between Flemish and Walloon regions.

Regional Elections (2014) - Marked growing support for regionalism and autonomy movements, especially in Flanders.

CHAPTER 11

BELGIUM IN THE 21ST CENTURY

2000 - PRESENT

In the 21st century, Belgium continues to play a significant role both within Europe and on the global stage, while facing domestic challenges linked to migration, regional tensions and

BELGIUM'S ANTWERP TODAY

environmental policy. The country has been a steadfast member of key international organisations, such as the European Union (EU) and NATO, while also contending with its own internal divisions between Flanders and Wallonia. At the same time, Belgian society is evolving rapidly in response to globalisation, immigration and technological innovation, leading to greater multiculturalism and fostering innovation across a range of sectors. This area looks at Belgium's position in the European and global context, its social challenges and political tensions and the impact of multiculturalism and technological progress on its society.

BELGIUM IN THE EUROPEAN AND GLOBAL CONTEXT

Belgium has long held a prominent place within the European Union and international organisations, owing to both its strategic location and its historical commitment to multilateralism. Brussels, the capital of Belgium, is often referred to as the "capital of Europe," as it hosts the headquarters of key EU institutions, including the European Commission, the European Council and parts of the European Parliament. The city also serves as the headquarters of NATO, further cementing its importance in international diplomacy and defence.

HEADQUARTERS OF NATO IN BRUSSELS

Belgium's role within the EU has been pivotal in shaping European integration. As one of the founding members of the European Economic Community (EEC), which later evolved into the European Union, Belgium has consistently championed European unity, supporting initiatives aimed at deepening cooperation between member states. The country has played an active role in promoting policies related to the single market, environmental sustainability and social cohesion, while also advocating for stronger governance at the EU level. Belgium's leadership in European diplomacy is underscored by its frequent involvement in EU negotiations and its willingness to mediate between larger member states during periods of political tension.

Beyond the EU, Belgium is a key player in global diplomacy through its membership in NATO and its participation in international organisations such as the United Nations (UN) and the World Trade Organisation (WTO). Belgium contributes to global peacekeeping missions and is a proponent of international law, human rights and humanitarian aid. It has also been active in global efforts to combat climate change, aligning itself with EU-wide initiatives to reduce carbon emissions and promote renewable energy sources.

SOCIAL CHALLENGES AND POLITICAL TENSIONS

Belgium faces a range of social and political challenges in the 21st century, many of which are linked to broader global trends such as migration, climate change and economic inequality. At the domestic level, the country continues to grapple with the ongoing tensions between Flanders and Wallonia, which remain a central feature of Belgian politics.

The linguistic and regional divide between the Dutch-speaking Flemish community and the French-speaking Walloon community has shaped Belgium's political landscape for decades. While the federal system established in the late 20th century granted significant autonomy to the regions, tensions over issues such as fiscal policy, social spending and economic development persist. Flanders, which has a stronger economy and lower unemployment than Wallonia, continues to push for greater fiscal autonomy, arguing that it should not be required to subsidise the less prosperous south. In contrast, Wallonia favours maintaining federal support and redistribution mechanisms to address regional disparities. These differing political and economic priorities have led to frequent government gridlock, with coalition governments often taking months to form due to the fragmented political landscape.

Migration is another significant challenge for Belgium, as it is for many European countries. In recent years, Belgium has experienced an influx of immigrants and refugees, particularly from Africa and the Middle East. While immigration has contributed to the country's multiculturalism and provided a vital source of labour, it has also led to social tensions and political debates over integration, asylum policy and the rise of far-right nationalist parties. The challenge of integrating new arrivals into Belgian society is compounded by the country's complex linguistic and regional divisions, with different communities adopting different approaches to immigration and multiculturalism.

THE MIGRATION ISSUE IN BELGIUM

Environmental policy is also a pressing concern for Belgium, particularly in the context of global efforts to address climate change. Belgium, like much of Europe, has set ambitious targets for reducing carbon emissions and transitioning to a more sustainable economy. However, the decentralised nature of the Belgian state means that environmental policies are often implemented at the regional level, leading to disparities in how Flanders, Wallonia and Brussels approach issues such as energy production, transport and urban development. This decentralisation has sometimes hindered the implementation of cohesive national policies, but Belgium remains committed to meeting EU climate goals and has made progress in areas such as renewable energy and waste management.

A Changing Society: Multiculturalism and Innovation

Belgian society in the 21st century is marked by increasing diversity, driven by immigration and globalisation. Belgium's multicultural character is especially evident in cities like Brussels and Antwerp, where large immigrant communities from Africa, the Middle East and Eastern Europe have settled. These communities have enriched Belgian society with new cultural influences, languages and traditions, contributing to a vibrant and dynamic social fabric. However, multiculturalism has also presented challenges, particularly in terms of social integration, housing and employment opportunities for immigrants and their descendants.

In response to these challenges, Belgium has implemented policies aimed at promoting social cohesion and inclusion. Education and employment programmes designed to integrate migrants and refugees into the workforce have been expanded, while local governments have taken steps to foster greater dialogue between communities. Belgium's experience with multiculturalism is reflective of broader European trends, as countries across the continent grapple with how to manage the social and economic impacts of migration in an increasingly globalised world.

In addition to its growing diversity, Belgium is also at the forefront of technological innovation and economic transformation. The country has positioned itself as a leader in sectors such as biotechnology, pharmaceuticals and information technology, with a strong focus on research and development. Belgium's universities and research institutions are highly regarded, attracting international talent and fostering collaboration with industry leaders. The country's commitment to innovation is also evident in its support for start-ups and small businesses, which have flourished in areas such as fintech, green energy and digital services.

The rise of innovation is not limited to the tech sector. Belgium has embraced the concept of a circular economy, focusing on sustainability, resource efficiency and reducing waste. This approach is particularly evident in industries such as construction and manufacturing, where

Belgian companies have developed cutting-edge techniques to minimise environmental impact while improving productivity. The country's embrace of technological change and sustainability reflects its broader commitment to addressing the challenges of the 21st century, while also ensuring that it remains competitive in the global economy.

SUMMARY:

In the 21st century, Belgium continues to be a key player in European and international politics, hosting institutions like the European Union and NATO. Domestically, Belgium faces challenges related to federalism, with ongoing debates over further regional autonomy. Economic inequality between the regions, migration and environmental concerns have also become major political issues. In recent years, Belgium has worked on balancing its internal divisions while maintaining its role as a leader in international diplomacy and cooperation.

DID YOU KNOW?

In 2011, Belgium set a world record by going 541 days without a government. Due to deep political divides between Flanders and Wallonia, Belgium went through an extended political crisis, eventually forming a coalition government after a year and a half without one.

Key People, Places and Events of the Era

PEOPLE:

King Philippe (b. 1960) - Current monarch, ascended to the throne in 2013.

Charles Michel (b. 1975) - Prime Minister of Belgium (2014–2019), now President of the European Council.

Sophie Wilmès (b. 1975) - Belgium's first female prime minister (2019–2020).

PLACES:

Brussels - Continues to serve as the capital of the EU and home to NATO.

Molenbeek - District in Brussels associated with radicalisation and the 2016 terrorist attacks.

EVENTS:

Brussels Terrorist Attacks (2016) - Coordinated bombings at Brussels Airport and a metro station, carried out by ISIS militants.

Ongoing Federal Reforms (2000s–present) - Continued efforts to balance regional autonomy with national unity, particularly between Flanders and Wallonia.

COVID- 19 Pandemic (2020) - Belgium was heavily impacted, with the government implementing strict lockdowns and public health measures.

CHAPTER 12

CULTURAL AND ARTISTIC HERITAGE

ALL TIMES PAST AND PRESENT

*B*elgium has a long and distinguished tradition of contributing to the world's cultural and artistic landscape. From its medieval masters who shaped Gothic architecture and Renaissance painting to the avant-garde movements of the 20th

BELGIAN CULTURAL HERITAGE

century, Belgium has consistently been at the forefront of artistic innovation. The country's unique cultural blend, shaped by its position between Latin and Germanic Europe, has produced a rich network of artistic expression, from Flemish Primitives to surrealist masterpieces. In more recent times, Belgium has made its mark in the realms of comics, cinema and popular culture, cementing its reputation as a hub of creativity and innovation. Belgium's cultural and artistic heritage, from the medieval and Renaissance periods to modernism, avant-garde art and contemporary culture will be explored in this chapter.

FROM MEDIEVAL MASTERS TO RENAISSANCE ART

Belgium's artistic legacy begins with the great medieval and Renaissance masters who laid the foundations for much of Western European art. During the Middle Ages, the region that is now Belgium was known for its extraordinary Gothic architecture. The construction of magnificent cathedrals, such as the Cathedral of Our Lady in Antwerp and the Saint Bavo Cathedral in Ghent, showcased the technical brilliance and spiritual ambition of Belgian architects and artisans. These towering edifices, with their intricate stonework and stained-glass windows, remain iconic examples of Gothic design and continue to attract visitors from around the world.

THE CATHEDRAL OF OUR LADY IN ANTWERP

In painting, Belgium's influence reached its zenith during the Renaissance with the rise of the Flemish Primitives, a group of artists known for their meticulous attention to detail and innovative use of oil paints. One of the most renowned figures of this movement was Jan van Eyck, whose masterpiece, 'The Arnolfini Portrait', revolutionised the use of oil painting with its remarkable realism and symbolism. Van Eyck and his contemporaries, such as Rogier van der Weyden and Hans Memling, were instrumental in shaping the early Northern Renaissance, influencing artists across Europe with their use of light, texture and perspective.

As the Renaissance progressed, Pieter Bruegel the Elder emerged as one of Belgium's most celebrated artists. Known for his landscapes and depictions of peasant life, Bruegel's works, such as 'The Tower of Babel' and 'The Peasant Wedding', offered vivid snapshots of 16th-century life while also conveying moral and philosophical themes. His detailed and often humorous depictions of everyday scenes made his work accessible to a broad audience and his influence can be seen in the later development of Dutch and Flemish painting. Bruegel's contribution to the art world marks one of the high points of Belgium's cultural history, bridging the medieval and modern eras.

MODERNISM AND THE AVANT-GARDE

Belgium's contribution to modernism and avant-garde art is equally significant, particularly through the work of surrealist artists such as René Magritte. A leading figure in the surrealist movement, Magritte is renowned for his thought-provoking, often paradoxical images that challenge the viewer's perception of reality. His works, such as 'The Treachery of Images' (the famous "This is not a pipe" painting) and 'The Son of Man' (a man with an apple obscuring his face), explore themes of identity, language and the tension between appearance and reality. Magritte's playful yet deeply philosophical approach to art has had a lasting impact on contemporary art, influencing not only painters but also filmmakers and writers.

The avant-garde spirit in Belgium was not confined to painting. During the early 20th century, Belgium became a centre for innovation in literature, theatre and design. The country's proximity to France and

Germany, two of the key centres of European avant-garde thought, allowed Belgian artists and intellectuals to engage with the latest movements, from Dadaism to constructivism. Belgian poets such as Paul van Ostaijen pushed the boundaries of literary form with their experiments in free verse and typographic design, while architect Victor Horta pioneered the Art Nouveau movement with his organic, flowing designs that broke away from traditional architectural styles. Horta's buildings, such as the Hôtel Tassel in Brussels, are considered masterpieces of early modern architecture, blending artistic creativity with functional design.

HORTA'S HÔTEL TASSEL IN BRUSSELS

Belgium's avant-garde legacy also includes the COBRA movement, a post-World War II group of artists and writers from Belgium, Denmark and the Netherlands. COBRA artists, such as Pierre Alechinsky, rejected formal academic training and embraced spontaneity, experimentation and collaboration, drawing inspiration from children's art, folk art and the unconscious mind. The movement's emphasis on freedom and creativity reflected the political and social upheavals of the post-war period and had a profound influence on European art in the latter half of the 20th century.

COMICS, CINEMA AND CONTEMPORARY CULTURE

In addition to its contributions to fine art, Belgium is also internationally renowned for its achievements in comics, cinema and popular culture. Belgium has long been a powerhouse in the world of comics, with 'bande dessinée' (Franco-Belgian comic strips) being a beloved art form in the country. One of Belgium's most famous cultural exports is 'The Adventures of Tintin', created by the cartoonist Hergé (Georges Remi) in 1929. Hergé's clear line drawing style, known as 'ligne claire', has influenced countless comic artists worldwide.

BELGIUM'S FAMOUS EXPORT 'THE ADVENTURE OF TINTIN'

Belgium is also home to other iconic comic book characters, such as 'The Smurfs' (created by Peyo) and 'Lucky Luke' (a Western comic created by Morris). These comics are not just children's entertainment but are also deeply embedded in Belgian culture, often reflecting the country's wit, humour and nuanced social commentary. Comic book art is celebrated across Belgium, with dedicated museums such as the Belgian Comic Strip Centre in Brussels, where visitors can explore the rich history and artistry behind these beloved stories.

In cinema, Belgium has produced several acclaimed filmmakers who have made significant contributions to both European and global cinema. The Dardenne brothers, Jean-Pierre and Luc, are among the most prominent contemporary Belgian filmmakers, known for their realist style and focus on social issues such as poverty, immigration and the struggles of the working class. Their films, including 'Rosetta' and 'The Child', have won multiple awards at international film festivals, including the prestigious Palme d'Or at the Cannes Film Festival. Belgium's film industry, while smaller in scale compared to Hollywood or the French film industry, punches above its weight in terms of artistic influence, with a focus on thoughtful, character-driven narratives.

JEAN-PIERRE AND LUC DARDENNE, PROMINENT CONTEMPORARY BELGIAN FILMMAKERS

Contemporary Belgian culture is also shaped by its dynamic music scene, with artists such as Stromae achieving international success with his fusion of electronic, pop and world music. Stromae's hit songs, such as 'Alors on danse' and 'Papaoutai', reflect the globalised, multicultural nature of Belgian society, blending French-language lyrics with diverse musical influences. Belgian electronic music has also made waves globally, with festivals like Tomorrowland in Boom becoming a premier destination for electronic dance music (EDM) enthusiasts from around the world.

SUMMARY:

Belgium's cultural and artistic heritage is a testament to its long history of creativity, innovation and influence. From the medieval masters who shaped Gothic architecture and Renaissance painting to the modernist and avant-garde movements of the 20th century, Belgium has consistently contributed to the evolution of European art. Its influence extends beyond the fine arts, with Belgium making a significant mark in the realms of comics, cinema and contemporary popular culture. Whether through the surrealist visions of René Magritte, the timeless adventures of Tintin, or the socially conscious films of the Dardenne brothers, Belgium's artistic legacy continues to inspire and resonate on a global scale.

DID YOU KNOW?

The comic strip "The Adventures of Tintin" was created by Belgian artist Hergé and has sold over 250 million copies worldwide. Belgium has a rich tradition of comic art, with many iconic characters such as Tintin and The Smurfs, reflecting the country's influential role in popular culture and the arts.

CONCLUSION

KEY LESSONS AND THEMES FROM BELGIUM'S HISTORY

FORTRESS IN ANTWERP

Belgium's rich and complex history offers valuable lessons about resilience, diversity and adaptability. Over the centuries, Belgium has evolved from a patchwork of medieval duchies into a modern federal state at the heart of Europe, navigating invasions, revolutions and profound social changes along the way. Key historical developments have shaped its unique national identity and political role.

One of the most striking lessons from Belgium's past is the country's capacity for balancing competing cultural, linguistic and regional identities. From its medieval origins as part of the Burgundian and Habsburg realms, through to its experience of division during the Reformation and subsequent religious wars, Belgium has always been a land of diverse influences. The coexistence of the Flemish and Walloon communities, as well as the smaller German-speaking minority, demonstrates Belgium's ability to accommodate difference while maintaining a sense of national unity. The transition to federalism in the 20th century, which granted greater autonomy to Flanders, Wallonia and

Brussels, is a testament to this balancing act, allowing Belgium to function effectively despite its internal divisions.

Another important historical theme is Belgium's role as a crossroads of European power struggles. Its strategic location between France, Germany and the Low Countries made it a battleground during major conflicts such as the Napoleonic Wars and the World Wars. Despite these challenges, Belgium emerged as a resilient nation, rebuilding itself after devastation and playing a crucial role in post-war European integration. The Belgian Revolution of 1830, which led to its independence, further exemplifies the nation's struggle for self-determination and sovereignty amid the competing interests of larger powers.

Belgium's commitment to diplomacy and internationalism is another key takeaway. Its role in founding the European Union, hosting EU institutions in Brussels and participating in NATO and other international organisations reflects Belgium's belief in multilateralism and cooperation as a path to peace and stability. This tradition of diplomacy is rooted in the country's historical experiences, particularly its vulnerability to external forces and its need to forge alliances to safeguard its interests.

BELGIUM'S FUTURE IN A GLOBALISED WORLD

As Belgium looks to the future, it faces several challenges and opportunities within an increasingly globalised and interconnected world. One of the most pressing issues is the ongoing tension between its regions, particularly Flanders and Wallonia. The linguistic and economic divide between the two communities remains a significant factor in Belgian politics and debates over further devolution or even the possibility of secession continues to shape the country's political discourse. The challenge for Belgium will be to maintain national unity while addressing the differing priorities and aspirations of its regions. The success of its federal system will depend on its ability to adapt to these internal tensions while ensuring that all communities feel represented and valued within the national framework.

Belgium's future is also closely tied to its role within the European Union. As one of the founding members of the EU, Belgium has long been a proponent of deeper integration and has played a key role in shaping the EU's institutions and policies. However, the EU itself faces challenges, from economic inequality between member states to the rise of populism and Euroscepticism in certain parts of the continent. Belgium, with its tradition of diplomacy and consensus-building, is well-positioned to continue playing a mediating role within the EU, helping to navigate these challenges while promoting unity and cooperation. Moreover, Brussels' status as the de facto capital of Europe ensures that Belgium will remain at the centre of European politics and diplomacy in the years to come.

BELGIUM IS FIRMLY TIED TO EUROPE

On the global stage, Belgium's future will be shaped by its responses to issues such as migration, environmental sustainability and technological innovation. As a small but influential nation, Belgium will need to balance its domestic priorities with its international responsibilities. The country's commitment to addressing climate change, fostering economic innovation and integrating immigrant communities will be crucial in determining its future success in an increasingly interconnected and competitive world.

SUMMARY:

Belgium's place in world history is defined by its ability to adapt, its commitment to diplomacy and its role as a mediator between diverse interests. As it faces the challenges of the 21st century, Belgium can draw on the lessons of its past to navigate a future that is both uncertain and full of potential. Whether through its leadership in the European Union, its efforts to balance regional autonomy with national unity, or its contributions to global diplomacy remain proactive.

Belgium's history is marked by its complex political structures, cultural developments and significant historical events. The following glossary provides explanations of key terms and concepts that are crucial to understanding Belgian history.

Burgundian Netherlands - The Burgundian Netherlands refers to the territories in the Low Countries that were under the rule of the Dukes of Burgundy from the late 14th to the early 16th centuries. This period is notable for its political and economic stability, as well as for its contributions to art and culture during the Renaissance. The Burgundian Netherlands played a crucial role in shaping the political landscape of modern Belgium and the Netherlands.

Habsburg Netherlands - The Habsburg Netherlands were the regions in the Low Countries that came under the control of the Habsburg dynasty in the early 16th century and remained under their rule until the late 18th century. This period included significant events such as the Eighty Years' War, which led to the separation of the northern provinces and the creation of the Dutch Republic, while the southern provinces remained under Habsburg control, contributing to the formation of modern Belgium.

Eighty Years' War (1568-1648) - The Eighty Years' War was a prolonged conflict between the Spanish Crown and the Protestant Dutch provinces. The war was driven by religious, political and economic tensions and ultimately resulted in the independence of the Dutch Republic from Spanish rule. The conflict had profound effects on the Low Countries, leading to the division between the northern and southern regions, with the southern part becoming part of the Spanish Habsburg territories.

Union of the Crowns (1815-1830) - The Union of the Crowns refers to the period when Belgium and the Netherlands were united under a single monarch, King William I, following the Congress of Vienna in 1815. This union was established to stabilise the region after the Napoleonic Wars. However, political and cultural differences between the Dutch-speaking northern regions and the French-speaking southern regions led to growing tensions, ultimately resulting in the Belgian Revolution and Belgium's independence in 1830.

Belgian Revolution (1830) - The Belgian Revolution was the uprising that led to Belgium's independence from the United Kingdom of the Netherlands and was driven by linguistic, economic and political grievances. The successful revolution resulted in the establishment of Belgium as a sovereign state and its own constitutional monarchy under King Leopold I.

Flemish Movement - The Flemish Movement is a cultural and political movement advocating for the rights and recognition of the Dutch-speaking Flemish population within Belgium. This movement has been instrumental in promoting the use of the Flemish language, cultural autonomy and regional political power. It played a key role in the development of Belgium's federal system and the establishment of linguistic and regional boundaries.

Walloon Region - The Walloon Region is the predominantly French-speaking southern part of Belgium. It has its own distinct cultural and linguistic identity. The Walloon Region's historical and economic development has significantly influenced Belgian politics, particularly in the context of federalism and regional autonomy.

Flanders - Flanders is the predominantly Dutch-speaking northern region of Belgium. It is an economically and culturally significant area within the country. The region has a strong sense of identity and has been a major player in Belgium's political and cultural landscape, including its role in the development of Belgium's federal system.

Brussels-Capital Region - The Brussels-Capital Region is one of Belgium's three federal regions, containing the capital city, Brussels. It is officially bilingual, with both French and Dutch being used. Brussels serves as the administrative and political centre of Belgium and the European Union, making it a pivotal location in both national and international affairs.

Treaty of London (1839) - The Treaty of London was an international agreement that recognised Belgium's independence and neutrality. Signed by the major European powers, this treaty established Belgium's status as a neutral state and defined its borders, which helped to secure its position in European diplomacy and international relations.

World War I and the Battle of Waterloo - World War I (1914-1918) saw Belgium invaded and occupied by German forces, leading to significant destruction and suffering. The Battle of Waterloo, fought in 1815, was a decisive conflict in which Napoleon Bonaparte was defeated by a coalition of European forces. Both events had profound impacts on Belgium, influencing its national identity and its role in European and global politics.

Federalism - Federalism is a system of government where power is divided between a central authority and regional or provincial governments. Belgium's federal structure, established in the late 20th century, accommodates its linguistic and regional diversity, granting significant autonomy to the regions of Flanders, Wallonia and Brussels. This system aims to balance regional interests with national governance.

Belgian Congo - The Belgian Congo was a colony in Central Africa controlled by Belgium from 1908 to 1960. The colony was a major source of wealth for Belgium, but it was also marked by severe exploitation and human rights abuses. The legacy of colonial rule continues to affect relations between Belgium and the Democratic Republic of the Congo.

Euroscepticism - Euroscepticism refers to the political stance opposed to the European Union or European integration. This sentiment has influenced Belgian politics, especially in regions with strong regional identities and differing views on European integration. Euroscepticism reflects broader debates about national sovereignty and the role of the EU in domestic affairs.

This timeline captures significant events in Belgian history, illustrating the country's development from ancient times through its modern era and into its future prospects.

c. 5000-2500 BCE - Early Neolithic settlements appear in Belgium, with evidence of agriculture and permanent settlements.

c. 2500-800 BCE - The Bronze Age in Belgium sees the development of metalworking and complex societies, with the construction of megalithic monuments.

c. 800 BCE-1 - The Iron Age brings the establishment of various tribes, including the Eburones and the Nervii, in what is now Belgium.

57 BCE - Julius Caesar conquers the region, incorporating it into the Roman Empire as part of Gallia Belgica.

1 CE - The Roman province of Gallia Belgica is formally established, leading to the development of infrastructure and urban centres.

275 CE - The region experiences invasions and instability during the later Roman Empire, leading to a decline in Roman control.

406 - The crossing of the Rhine by various Germanic tribes, including the Vandals, Alans and Suebi, marks the end of Roman rule in Belgica.

486 - Clovis I, King of the Franks, unifies the Frankish tribes and establishes control over the region, marking the beginning of the Merovingian dynasty.

751 - Pepin the Short is crowned King of the Franks, initiating the Carolingian dynasty and beginning the Carolingian Empire.

843 - The Treaty of Verdun divides the Carolingian Empire among Charlemagne's grandsons, with parts of what is now Belgium falling under West Francia and Middle Francia.

11th-12th Centuries - The region experiences significant feudal development and the growth of powerful city-states and principalities.

1185 - The Battle of Worringen sees the victory of the Duchy of Brabant over the Archbishop of Cologne, reinforcing Brabant's influence in the region.

1302 - The Battle of the Golden Spurs (Bataille des Éperons d'Or) occurs, where Flemish forces defeat the French army, marking a significant event in the struggle for Flemish independence.

1435 - The Treaty of Arras ends the conflict between the Burgundian Duke Philip the Good and the French crown, solidifying Burgundian control over much of Belgium.

1477 - The marriage of Mary of Burgundy to Maximilian I of Austria brings the Habsburgs into control of the Burgundian Netherlands.

1556 - Philip II of Spain inherits the Habsburg Netherlands, beginning the Spanish rule over the region.

1648 - The Treaty of Münster ends the Eighty Years' War, formally recognising the independence of the Dutch Republic and placing the southern Netherlands under Spanish control.

1713 - The Treaty of Utrecht concludes the War of Spanish Succession, with the southern Netherlands ceded to the Austrian Habsburgs, becoming known as the Austrian Netherlands.

1794 - Revolutionary France annexes the Austrian Netherlands, ending Habsburg rule and integrating the region into France.

1815 - The Congress of Vienna restores the region to Dutch control, merging it with the Kingdom of the Netherlands.

1830 - The Belgian Revolution leads to the independence of Belgium from the United Kingdom of the Netherlands.

1831 - Leopold I is inaugurated as the first King of Belgium, establishing the constitutional monarchy.

1835 - The opening of the first Belgian railway line marks the beginning of the Industrial Revolution in Belgium.

1885 - King Leopold II's acquisition of the Congo Free State, leading to a period of severe exploitation and colonisation.

1914-1918 - Belgium is invaded by Germany during World War I, experiencing extensive destruction and suffering throughout the conflict.

1940-1944 - Belgium is again invaded by Germany during World War II, with occupation lasting until Allied liberation in 1944.

1948 - Belgium becomes a founding member of the Benelux Union, a precursor to the European Union.

1951 - The European Coal and Steel Community is established, with Belgium as a founding member, leading to further European integration.

1970 - The first state reform establishes Belgium as a federal state, significantly decentralising powers to regions and communities.

2003 - Belgium legalises same-sex marriage, reflecting its progressive social policies.

2016 - Brussels is targeted by terrorist attacks, highlighting issues related to security and international terrorism.

2020s - The country continues to play a significant role in European and global affairs while addressing internal and external issues.

APPENDIX 3: NOTABLE RULERS IN BELGIUM'S HISTORY

This timeline includes key rulers and leaders who have significantly influenced Belgium's history from the pre-Roman era through modern times.

PRE-ROMAN AND ROMAN PERIODS

Celtic Tribal Chiefs (Pre-Roman Era) - Various tribal leaders ruled the region before Roman conquest, including leaders of tribes like the Eburones and Nervii.

Julius Caesar (100-44 BCE) - Roman general who conquered and integrated the region into the Roman Empire as part of Gallia Belgica.

MEROVINGIAN AND CAROLINGIAN PERIODS

Clovis I (c. 466-511) - King of the Franks who unified the Frankish tribes and began the process of Christianisation in the region.

Charles Martel (c. 688-741) - Frankish leader who defeated the Muslim forces at the Battle of Tours and consolidated Frankish power, influencing the region.

Pepin the Short (c. 714-768) - King of the Franks who initiated the Carolingian dynasty and was pivotal in establishing Carolingian rule.

Charlemagne (c. 742-814) - Emperor of the Carolingian Empire whose reign marked significant cultural and administrative developments in the region.

Philip the Bold (1342-1404) - Duke of Burgundy who greatly expanded Burgundian territories, including the area of modern Belgium, enhancing its political influence.

Mary of Burgundy (1457-1482) - Duchess of Burgundy whose marriage to Maximilian I of Austria integrated the Burgundian inheritance into the Habsburg dynasty.

Charles V (1500-1558) - Holy Roman Emperor and King of Spain whose vast empire included the Low Countries and greatly influenced Belgian affairs.

Spanish and Austrian Netherlands

Philip II of Spain (1527-1598) - King of Spain who ruled the Southern Netherlands, facing resistance and conflict with the Protestant northern provinces.

Leopold I (1790-1865) - First King of the Belgians, inaugurated in 1831 after Belgium's independence from the United Kingdom of the Netherlands.

Albert I (1875-1934) - King of Belgium during World War I, known for his leadership and resistance during the German occupation.

Modern Period

Leopold II (1835-1909) - King of Belgium who is infamous for his exploitation and brutal rule over the Congo Free State, which was his personal possession.

Baudouin I (1930-1993) - King of Belgium who reigned from 1951 to 1993 and played a stabilising role in post-war Belgium, overseeing significant social and economic changes.

Albert II (1934-) - King of Belgium who reigned from 1993 to 2013, known for his role in modernising Belgium and addressing political and social issues.

Philippe (1960-) - Current King of Belgium, who ascended the throne in 2013, continuing the role of the Belgian monarchy in contemporary European and Belgian affairs.

CONTEMPORARY LEADERS

Sophie Wilmès (1975-) - First female Prime Minister of Belgium (2019-2020), known for her leadership during the COVID-19 pandemic.

This list highlights key figures in the Belgian arts across various periods, showcasing the country's rich cultural heritage and influential contributions to global arts.

EARLY MODERN PERIOD

Pieter Bruegel the Elder (c. 1525-1569) - Renowned Flemish painter known for his detailed landscapes and peasant scenes, such as "The Peasant Wedding" and "The Triumph of Death."

Peter Paul Rubens (1577-1640) - Celebrated Baroque painter whose dynamic compositions and vibrant works include "The Descent from the Cross" and "The Adoration of the Magi."

Antoine van Dyck (1599-1641) - Flemish portrait painter and a prominent student of Rubens, noted for his elegant and expressive portraits of aristocracy.

19TH CENTURY

James Ensor (1860-1949) - Belgian painter known for his expressionistic and often grotesque works, including "The Entry of Christ into Brussels" and "The Skeletons Fight Back."

Maurice Maeterlinck (1862-1949) - Belgian playwright and poet who won the Nobel Prize in Literature in 1911 for his symbolist plays such as "Pelléas and Mélisande."

René Magritte (1898-1967) - Influential surrealist painter famous for his thought-provoking and enigmatic works, including "The Treachery of Images" and "The Lovers."

Hergé (1907-1983) - Pseudonym of Georges Remi, the creator of the beloved comic series "The Adventures of Tintin," which has been widely acclaimed for its storytelling and detailed artwork.

Marc Sleen (1922-2006) - Belgian comic artist known for his popular series "De Snoegrens," contributing significantly to Belgian comic culture.

André Delvaux (1926-2002) - Belgian film director and screenwriter known for his films such as "The Man Who Had His Hair Cut Short" and "The Tango of the Devil," which have been influential in Belgian cinema.

CONTEMPORARY PERIOD

Amélie Nothomb (1966-) - Belgian author renowned for her novels such as "Hygiene and the Assassin" and "The Character of Rain," known for her distinctive style and critical acclaim.

Sophie Nélisse (1996-) - Belgian actress recognised for her roles in films such as "The Book Thief" and "Monsieur Lazhar," gaining international attention for her performances.

Stromae (1985-) - Belgian singer, songwriter and record producer known for his innovative music blending electronic, hip-hop and pop influences, with hits like "Alors on danse" and "Papaoutai."

Eddy Merckx (1945-) - Although primarily known as a cyclist, Merckx's involvement in Belgian culture and his contributions to sports as a form of artistic performance are noteworthy.

APPENDIX 5: NOTABLE BELGIAN INNOVATORS AND SCIENTISTS

This timeline features influential Belgians who have made significant contributions to the fields of invention, science and technology, showcasing Belgium's rich history of innovation and discovery.

EARLY MODERN AND 19TH CENTURY

Adolphe Sax (1814-1894) - Belgian inventor and musician best known for inventing the saxophone, a versatile brass instrument that has become integral to various music genres.

Lieven Bauwens (1773-1822) - Belgian industrialist who played a key role in bringing the Industrial Revolution to Belgium by establishing the first mechanised cotton spinning mill.

Joseph Plateau (1801-1883) - Belgian physicist known for his work in the study of visual perception and the invention of the phenakistoscope, an early motion picture device.

Jean-Baptiste Andre Godin (1817-1888) - Belgian inventor and industrialist famous for developing the "Godin" cast iron stoves and creating a model of industrial and social utopia in the form of the Familistère de Guise.

20TH CENTURY

Georges Lemaître (1894-1966) - Belgian astrophysicist and priest who proposed the theory of the "primeval atom," which later became known as the Big Bang Theory, fundamentally shaping modern cosmology.

Pierre-Denis (1888-1956) - Belgian chemist known for his research in organic chemistry and the synthesis of complex chemical compounds, contributing to advancements in chemical science.

André-Marie Ampère (1775-1836) - Although not Belgian, Ampère's contributions to electromagnetism heavily influenced Belgian scientists and engineers in their work on electrical phenomena.

Paul-Henri Spaak (1899-1972) - Belgian politician and statesman who, while not a scientist, was instrumental in shaping the European Community's policies, which have influenced scientific cooperation and development in Europe.

CONTEMPORARY PERIOD

Marc Van Montagu (1933-) - Belgian biotechnologist who, along with Jeff Schell, developed techniques for genetic engineering in plants, contributing significantly to modern agricultural biotechnology.

Jean-Pierre Sauvage (1944-) - Belgian chemist who was awarded the Nobel Prize in Chemistry in 2016 for his work in supramolecular chemistry, which involves the design and synthesis of complex molecular structures.

Francois Barre-Sinoussi (1947-) - Belgian-born French virologist who, along with Luc Montagnier, discovered the HIV virus, which has had a profound impact on the understanding and treatment of AIDS.

Benoît Mandlebrot (1924-2010) - Although born in France, Mandlebrot's work in fractal geometry was influenced by Belgian mathematicians and has had a global impact on various scientific fields, including the study of complex systems.

Tijl De Bie (1986-) - Belgian scientist known for his work in machine learning and artificial intelligence, contributing to advancements in data science and computational technologies.

APPENDIX 6: HERITAGE AND TRADITIONS OF BELGIUM

These traditions and heritage elements showcase Belgium's cultural diversity, blending influences from its Flemish, Walloon and Brussels communities, as well as its historical connections with neighbouring countries.

Carnival of Binche - The Carnival of Binche is one of Belgium's most famous folk festivals, celebrated before Lent. Dating back to the 14th century, it features masked participants called "Gilles" who wear elaborate costumes and throw oranges into the crowd as a symbol of good luck. Recognised by UNESCO as a Masterpiece of the Oral and Intangible Heritage of Humanity, this vibrant event is a highlight of Belgian culture.

Ommegang Pageant - The Ommegang Pageant in Brussels re-enacts the entry of Emperor Charles V into the city in 1549. Held every July, this historic procession features participants in period costumes, traditional dances, horseback displays and music, celebrating the city's medieval history.

Belgium's Beer Culture - Belgium is renowned for its beer culture, boasting over 1,500 different types of beer. The brewing tradition dates back to the Middle Ages, with Trappist and Abbey beers being particularly noteworthy. In 2016, UNESCO recognised Belgian beer culture as an Intangible Cultural Heritage, underscoring its importance to the nation's identity.

Saint Nicholas Day (Sinterklaas) - Saint Nicholas Day, celebrated on 6th December, is particularly popular in the Flemish-speaking parts of Belgium. Children receive gifts from Sinterklaas, who is accompanied by his helper, Zwarte Piet. This tradition, similar to Christmas, holds a distinct place in Belgian culture.

Ducasse de Mons (Doudou) - The Ducasse de Mons, also known as Doudou, is a centuries-old festival celebrated in the town of Mons on Trinity Sunday. The highlight is the re-enactment of Saint George's fight with the dragon, symbolising the triumph of good over evil. Recognised by UNESCO, this festival is a cherished part of Belgium's heritage.

Meiboomplanting (May Tree Planting) - Meiboomplanting is a traditional celebration in Brussels, held annually on 9th August. The event includes a parade and the planting of a symbolic "May Tree," believed to bring good fortune to the city. This tradition, rooted in medieval legend, continues to be celebrated with great enthusiasm.

Belgium's Lace-making Tradition - Lace-making has been a significant craft in Belgium, with Brussels, Bruges and Mechelen being key centres. Belgian lace became highly prized in the 17th century, known for its intricate designs and fine craftsmanship. Today, lace remains a symbol of Belgium's artistic heritage.

Belgian Chocolate - Belgian chocolate is world-renowned for its quality and variety, with a history dating back to the 17th century. The country is famous for its pralines and truffles and the tradition of fine chocolate-making continues to be a significant part of Belgian culture and identity.

Folklore and Giants - In many Belgian towns, folklore parades featuring giant puppets, known as "Reuzen" in Dutch or "Géants" in French, are a popular tradition. These giants represent historical or mythical figures and are carried through the streets during local festivals, symbolising the community's heritage.

Procession of the Holy Blood - The Procession of the Holy Blood, held in Bruges every Ascension Day, involves a relic said to contain the blood of Christ being paraded through the streets. Celebrated since the 13th century, this event is a significant religious and cultural tradition in Belgium.

Feast of Saint Martin - The Feast of Saint Martin, celebrated on 11th November, is especially popular in the eastern regions of Belgium. Children go door-to-door singing songs and receiving sweets, similar to

Halloween. The day honours the charitable deeds of Saint Martin and is marked with various local customs and festivities.

Walloon Festival - The Walloon Festival, held in September in the Walloon region, is a celebration of Walloon identity and culture. The festival features music, dance and traditional games, promoting the region's French-speaking heritage.

End-of-Year Festivities - Belgium's end-of-year festivities blend religious observances with folklore. Christmas markets, elaborate decorations and festive foods like "cougnou" (a sweet bread) are central to the celebrations, which include both Christmas and New Year traditions.

Zinneke Parade - The Zinneke Parade in Brussels is a biennial multicultural and artistic event that showcases the city's diversity. With elaborate floats, costumes and performances, the parade reflects the contemporary cultural heritage of Brussels' population.

Art Nouveau Architecture - Art Nouveau architecture is a significant aspect of Belgium's heritage, particularly in Brussels. Architects like Victor Horta and Henry van de Velde were pioneers of this style in the late 19th and early 20th centuries, creating buildings characterised by intricate ironwork, flowing lines and organic forms.

National Day Celebrations - Belgium's National Day, celebrated on 21st July, commemorates the inauguration of King Leopold I, the country's first monarch, in 1831. The day is marked by parades, fireworks and various cultural events across Belgium, celebrating national unity and independence.

Manneken Pis - +The Manneken Pis, a small statue of a boy urinating, is one of Brussels' most famous symbols. Dating back to the 17th century, the statue has numerous legends associated with it and is often dressed in costumes for special occasions, reflecting the quirky and humorous side of Belgian culture.

Poppies and Remembrance - Poppies and remembrance play a significant role in Belgium's commemoration of World War I. The battles of Ypres, in particular, are key sites of remembrance. The poppy, immortalised in the poem "In Flanders Fields," is a symbol used to remember those who died in the war, especially on Armistice Day, 11th November.

Mardi Gras in Malmedy - The Mardi Gras in Malmedy is a unique version of the festival celebrated in the Walloon region. The four-day event includes parades, masked balls and traditional performances, reflecting local folklore and customs.

Saint Véronique Festival - The Saint Véronique Festival in Bouillon features a dramatic re-enactment of the Passion of Christ, with participants taking on roles in the Biblical narrative. This tradition highlights the deep-rooted religious and communal heritage in the region.

Tintin: Belgium's Iconic Comic - Tintin, the iconic comic book character created by Hergé, is a symbol of Belgian culture and creativity. Since 1929, Tintin and his dog Snowy have captivated audiences worldwide. Tintin's adventures are celebrated in museums, exhibitions and festivals, making him an enduring part of Belgium's cultural heritage.

APPENDIX 7: LEGENDS OF BELGIUM SPORT

This list highlights Belgium's rich sporting heritage, showcasing athletes who have excelled on both the national and international stages.

Jacky Ickx - Date of Birth: 1 January 1945 - One of Belgium's most successful racing drivers, Jacky Ickx won eight Formula 1 Grand Prix races and six 24 Hours of Le Mans titles. He was also a two-time runner-up in the Formula 1 World Championship.

Eddy Merckx - Date of Birth: 17 June 1945 - Considered one of the greatest cyclists of all time. He dominated the sport, winning the Tour de France and Giro d'Italia five times each and the Vuelta a España once. His incredible success earned him the nickname "The Cannibal."

Jan Ceulemans - Date of Birth: 28 February 1957 - A football legend in Belgium, Jan Ceulemans earned over 90 caps for the national team, captaining Belgium during their successful campaigns in the 1982 and 1986 FIFA World Cups. He spent much of his club career at Club Brugge, where he won numerous domestic titles.

Thierry Boutsen - Date of Birth: 13 July 1957 - Competed in Formula 1 from 1983 to 1993, winning three Grand Prix races. He also found success in sports car racing, including a victory at the 24 Hours of Le Mans.

Jean-Michel Saive - Date of Birth: 17 November 1969 - One of Belgium's greatest table tennis players. He was a runner-up in the 1993 World Championships and spent 515 weeks in the top 10 of the world rankings. Saive also competed in seven Olympic Games.

Sven Nys - Date of Birth: 17 June 1976 - One of the most successful cyclo-cross riders in history, with two World Championship titles and a record seven World Cup overall wins. He also won the Belgian national championship nine times and was a two-time European Champion.

Tia Hellebaut - Date of Birth: 16 February 1978 - Made history by winning the gold medal in the high jump at the 2008 Beijing Olympics. She was also a European Indoor Champion and set a Belgian record with a jump of 2.05 metres.

Kim Gevaert - Date of Birth: 5 August 1978 - A former sprinter who won the gold medal in the 4x100m relay at the 2008 Beijing Olympics. She also claimed multiple European Championships in the 100m and 200m events, establishing herself as one of Belgium's top athletes.

Tom Boonen - Date of Birth: 15 October 1980 - Excelled in classic one-day races, winning Paris-Roubaix four times and the Tour of Flanders three times. He also won the World Road Race Championship in 2005 and enjoyed a successful career that included wearing the Tour de France yellow jersey.

Justine Henin - Date of Birth: 1 June 1982 - Regarded as one of the greatest female tennis players ever. She won seven Grand Slam singles titles, including four French Opens and an Olympic gold medal in 2004. Henin was known for her powerful backhand and mental toughness.

Philippe Gilbert - Date of Birth: 5 July 1982 - Known for his strength in one-day cycling races, having won all three Ardennes classics—Amstel Gold Race, La Flèche Wallonne and Liège-Bastogne-Liège. He also claimed the World Road Race Championship in 2012 and has stage wins in all three Grand Tours.

Kim Clijsters - Date of Birth: 8 June 1983 - Another of Belgium's tennis greats. She claimed four Grand Slam singles titles and two doubles titles during her career. Her powerful baseline game and athleticism made her a fan favourite and she achieved a remarkable comeback by winning the US Open in 2009 after retirement.

Greg Van Avermaet - Date of Birth: 17 May 1985 - Achieved significant success in cycling, including winning the gold medal in the men's road race at the 2016 Rio Olympics. He has also triumphed in Paris-Roubaix, the Tour of Flanders and has worn the yellow jersey in the Tour de France.

Vincent Kompany - Date of Birth: 10 April 1986 - A legendary figure in Belgian football. As a captain for Manchester City, he led the team to multiple Premier League victories. Kompany is celebrated for his leadership, defensive strength and crucial goals, both for his club and the Belgian national team.

David Goffin - Date of Birth: 7 December 1990 - The first Belgian male tennis player to reach the ATP top 10. Known for his consistency and solid play, he has reached the quarter-finals of several Grand Slam tournaments and was a runner-up in the 2017 ATP Finals.

Eden Hazard - Date of Birth: 7 January 1991 - One of Belgium's most celebrated footballers. He has played for top clubs like Lille, Chelsea and Real Madrid, where he won numerous league titles and domestic cups. Hazard played a key role in Belgium's impressive third-place finish at the 2018 FIFA World Cup.

Kevin De Bruyne - Date of Birth: 28 June 1991 - Known for his exceptional skills as a midfielder. He has been a crucial player for Manchester City, helping them secure multiple Premier League titles. De Bruyne's vision, passing and shooting ability also made him a standout performer for Belgium in the 2018 FIFA World Cup.

Romelu Lukaku - Date of Birth: 13 May 1993 - Belgium's all-time top scorer with over 70 international goals. His career includes stints at major clubs such as Chelsea, Manchester United, Inter Milan and Roma. Known for his strength and finishing prowess, Lukaku has established himself as one of the top strikers in football.

Nafissatou Thiam - Date of Birth: 19 August 1994 - A heptathlete who has brought great pride to Belgium. She won gold medals at both the 2016 Rio Olympics and the 2020 Tokyo Olympics. Thiam is also a two-time World Champion and a European Champion in the heptathlon.

For those interested in exploring the rich and complex history of Belgium, the following selection of books, articles, documentaries and online resources offers a deeper understanding of the country's past.

BOOKS

Belgium: Long United, Long Divided by Samuel Humes
This comprehensive book provides a thorough examination of Belgium's political and cultural history, exploring the tensions between the Flemish and Walloon regions and the nation's development from its foundation to modern times.

The Invention of Belgium: A History of a Small Country by Luc de Vos
An insightful look into the creation of Belgium, this book explores the historical, social and political forces that shaped the country and continue to influence it today.

A Throne in Brussels: Britain, the Saxe-Coburgs and the Belgianisation of Europe by Paul Belien
This provocative analysis delves into the role of the monarchy in Belgium and examines the influence of British and European politics on its formation and identity.

The Belgian Congo: Power and Struggle in a Colonial Context by Guy Vanthemsche
A focused study of Belgium's colonial history, this book investigates the political and economic consequences of Belgian rule in the Congo and the legacy of this era.

ARTICLES

The Belgian Revolution of 1830 by Michael Rapport
Published in History Today, this article provides a detailed account of the revolution that led to Belgium's independence from the Netherlands, a pivotal moment in European history.

The Linguistic Divide in Belgium by Rik Torfs
Featured in The European Journal of Language Policy, this article discusses the enduring language divide in Belgium and its implications for national identity and political stability.

Belgium's Role in the First World War by Sophie de Schaepdrijver
This article, published in The Journal of Military History, offers a critical look at Belgium's position during the First World War, focusing on its occupation and the impact on Belgian society.

DOCUMENTARIES

The Great War: The Invasion of Belgium
This documentary traces Belgium's role in the early stages of the First World War, focusing on the German invasion and the heroic defence by Belgian forces. It highlights the war's devastating effect on the Belgian people.

King Leopold's Ghost
Based on Adam Hochschild's book of the same name, this documentary investigates the atrocities committed in the Congo under King Leopold II's reign and explores the human and economic toll of Belgian colonialism.

The Belgian Legacy
A historical overview of Belgium's development, this documentary covers key moments in the nation's history, from its independence in 1830 to its role in international affairs and its internal political struggles.

Belgium: A History of Conflict and Compromise
This resource, provided by the BBC, offers an accessible summary of Belgium's history, focusing on key events such as its independence, the world wars and its contemporary political divisions.

Royal Museum for Central Africa
The official website of the Royal Museum for Central Africa offers extensive resources on Belgium's colonial past, including virtual exhibitions, scholarly articles and digitised archives related to Belgian Congo.

The Belgian Revolution – Encyclopaedia Britannica
An in-depth entry that provides an overview of the Belgian Revolution, its causes, key figures and outcomes, offering a concise yet informative exploration of this significant event.

Belgium's Role in World War II – The National WWII Museum
This resource provides detailed information on Belgium's occupation during the Second World War, including articles, maps and personal testimonies that shed light on the country's experiences during this period.

IMAGE CAPTION/Source

LOCATION OF BELGIUM IN EUROPE
www.maps-belgium.com
MAP OF BELGIUM
www.worldatlas.com
THE BELGIAN PEOPLE
www.0bknra.blogspot.com
CAVE PAINTINGS FOUND IN BELGIUM
www.vilters-vanhemel.be
NEANDERTHAL REMAINS FROM
THE REMAINS OF A ROMAN VILLA AT
METTET
www.villamageroy.com
MIDDLE AGE PEASANT LIFE
www.lifeinthemiddleages1.weebly.com
CHARLEMAGNE'S CAROLINGIAN EMPIRE
ENCOMPASSED MOST OF WESTERN
EUROPE
www.tonsoffacts.com
MAP OF THE BURGUNDY KINGDOM
www.mavink.com
SCENE PAINTED OF THE BATTLE OF
NANCY
www.alchetron.com
THE HABSBURG DYNASTY
www.historyextra.com
CHARLES V TRIED TO REFORM BUT WITH
CONFLICT
Public domain, via Wikimedia Commons
THE FRENCH RULE IN BELGIUM FROM
1794 -1815
www.britannica.com
THE NAPOLEONIC CIVIL CODE OF 1804
www.napoleon.org
AN ARTIST'S DEPICTION OF THE BELGIAN
REVOLUTION IN BRUSSELS
www.flickr.com
THE INDUSTRIAL REVOLUTION
www.atenor.eu

www.britannica.com
TYPICAL SCENE FROM AN INDUSTRIAL
SITE IN BELGIUM
www.timetoast.com
THE BELGIAN WORKERS' (POB) WAS
FOUNDED IN 1885
www.jacques-tourtaux-over-blog.com
BELGIUM'S SUFFERING DURING WORLD
WAR I
www.huffingtonpost.com
GERMAN RIDERS AND MOTORCYCLISTS
IN FRANCE IN 1940
www.ebay.com
ECSC MAP: BELGIUM WAS ONE OF THE
ORIGINAL MEMBERS IN 1951
www.germanculture.com.ua
MAP OF THE REGIONAL LANGUAGES IN
BELGIUM
www.polgeonow.com
HEADQUARTERS OF NATO IN BRUSSELS
www.sigzincandcopper.co.uk
THE MIGRATION ISSUE IN BELGIUM
www.investors.com
BELGIAN CULTURAL HERITAGE
www.insidebelgium.weebly.com
THE CATHEDRAL OF OUR LADY IN
ANTWERP
www.orangesmile
HORTA'S HÔTEL TASSEL IN BRUSSELS
www.es.wikiarquitectura.com
BELGIUM'S FAMOUS EXPORT 'THE
ADVENTURE OF TINTIN'
www.fanpop.com
FORTRESS IN ANTWERP
www.iexplore.com
BELGIUM IS FIRMLY TIED TO EUROPE

All other images are either Public Domain, via Wikimedia
Commons or Source Unknown

OTHER BOOKS IN THE SERIES AVAILABLE

CYPRUS THROUGH THE AGES

UKRAINE THROUGH THE AGES

BULGARIA THROUGH THE AGES

WALES THROUGH THE AGES

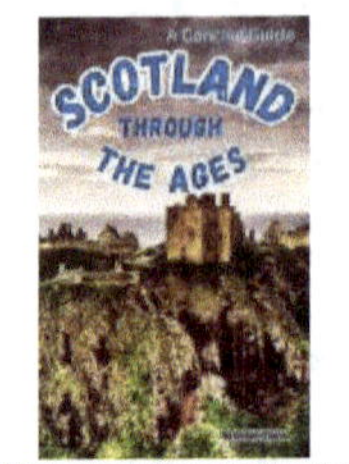

ICELAND THROUGH THE AGES

TURKEY THROUGH THE AGES

MALTA THROUGH THE AGES

SCOTLAND THROUGH THE AGES

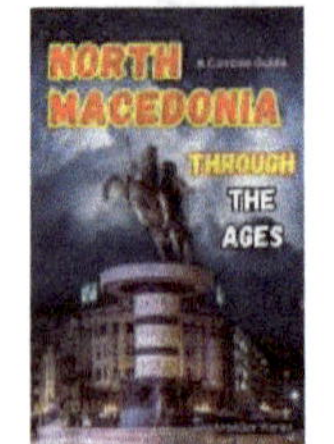

GREECE THROUGH THE AGES

SERBIA THROUGH THE AGES

FRANCE THROUGH THE AGES

NORTH MACEDONIA THROUGH THE AGES

ENGLAND THROUGH THE AGES

GIBRALTAR THROUGH THE AGES